MasterChef
Prepare
Ahead

MasterChef
Prepare
Ahead

Contents

Plate Up

Finishing Touches

Leave It Be

Plate Up

Sorrel soup with salmon and dill and oatcakes

Kirsty Wark @ Celebrity finalist

Preparation time 25 minutes   **Cooking time** 50 minutes   **Serves 4**

PREPARE AHEAD
Steps 1-5

Ingredients

For the vegetable stock

2 celery sticks, roughly chopped

2 carrots, roughly chopped

1 onion, roughly chopped

1 leek, roughly chopped

1 bay leaf

100g (3½oz) frozen peas

2 sprigs of thyme

salt and freshly ground black pepper

For the oatcakes

100g (3½oz) medium oatmeal

100g (3½oz) fine-ground oatmeal

pinch of bicarbonate of soda

2 tsp melted lard

plain flour, for dusting

For the soup

45g (1½oz) unsalted butter

1 onion, chopped

1 small potato, peeled and diced

1 tsp vitamin C powder

350g (12oz) sorrel, stalks removed and leaves chopped

1 small, round lettuce, leaves separated and chopped

20g (¾oz) chervil, chopped

900ml (1½ pints) vegetable stock

4–6 tbsp double cream

300g (10oz) fresh salmon fillet, skinned and diced

2 tbsp chopped dill

Method

1 For the stock, put all the vegetables and herbs in a heavy pan, cover with 900ml (1½ pints) water and season with salt and pepper. Bring to the boil and simmer for 30 minutes, then strain. Set aside until needed.

2 To make the oatcakes, preheat the oven to 160°C (325°F/Gas 3). Mix the dry ingredients together, add the lard and 3 tbsp of water, and draw together to form a dough.

3 Dust the work surface with flour and roll out the dough to a thickness of 5mm (¼in). Cut out rounds with a 6cm (2½in) biscuit cutter and transfer to a non-stick baking tray. Bake for 25 minutes until crisp, then leave to cool.

4 Meanwhile, make the soup. Melt the butter in a pan, then add the onion and potato and soften for 5 minutes – do not allow them to brown.

5 Add the vitamin C powder, sorrel, lettuce, and chervil and cook for 1–2 minutes until the leaves have wilted. Add the vegetable stock, then remove from the heat and purée in batches in a blender. Return to the pan, stir in the cream, and then season to taste. Set aside.

6 To serve, reheat soup and transfer to a jug. Combine the salmon and dill in a bowl, then divide between 4 soup bowls. Pour the hot soup around the salmon – the residual heat will be sufficient to cook it. Serve with the oatcakes.

Butternut squash soup

Nihal Arthanayake ⓜ **Celebrity contestant**

Preparation time 20 minutes   **Cooking time** 30 minutes   **Serves 4**

<table>
<tr><td>PREPARE AHEAD
Steps 1-3</td></tr>
</table>

Ingredients

25g (scant 1oz) butter

1 onion, chopped

1 butternut squash, approx. 1kg (2¼lb) in weight, deseeded and cut into large chunks

1 tsp ground cumin

750ml–1 litre (1¼–1¾ pints) chicken stock

salt and freshly ground black pepper

2–3 tbsp plain yogurt

Method

1 Melt the butter in a large saucepan. Add the onion and cook over medium heat, stirring, for 4–5 minutes until it has softened but not coloured.

2 Add the squash chunks with the ground cumin and cook for a further 1–2 minutes, stirring to coat.

3 Add the stock, bring to a simmer, and cook for 15–20 minutes or until the squash is tender. Purée using a hand blender or, for a smoother result, by transferring to a food processor in batches. Set aside.

4 Just before serving, reheat the soup, season to taste, and finally stir in the yogurt.

Tomato salad in a savoury tuile basket, topped with a basil sorbet

Tim Kinnaird @ finalist

Preparation time 30 minutes   **Cooking time** 15 minutes   **Serves 8**

PREPARE AHEAD
Steps 1-5

Ingredients

25g (scant 1oz) basil leaves, plus extra shredded leaves to garnish

7–8 tbsp extra virgin olive oil

32 red cherry tomatoes, peeled

16 yellow cherry tomatoes, peeled

For the sorbet

100g (3½oz) caster sugar

small bunch of basil leaves

squeeze of lemon juice

For the baskets

1 small garlic clove

pinch of coarse sea salt

50g (1¾oz) unsalted butter

30g (1oz) plain flour

2 tbsp caster sugar

1 large egg, white only

100g (3½oz) Parmesan cheese, finely grated

1 tbsp finely chopped rosemary leaves

Method →

Method

1 To make the sorbet, dissolve the sugar in 200ml (7fl oz) water over a moderate heat. Stir in the basil and lemon juice. Blend in a food processor, then pass through a fine sieve. Line a second sieve with muslin and set over a bowl. Pour in the basil syrup and leave to drain.

2 Pour the syrup into an ice-cream maker and churn until set. Line a baking tray with baking parchment. Using 2 dessert spoons shape quenelles of sorbet, place on the tray, and freeze.

3 To make the baskets, preheat the oven to 200°C (400°F/Gas 6). Lline 2 baking trays with baking parchment. Draw four 12cm (5in) circles on each sheet of baking parchment, well spaced apart. Grease the outsides of 8 medium dariole moulds and sit them upturned on another baking tray. Crush and mince the garlic to a fine paste with the sea salt using the back of a knife. Beat butter until pale and then beat in the flour, sugar, and garlic. Slowly beat in the egg white and Parmesan to form a sticky paste.

4 Dollop 2–3 teaspoons of the mixture into each circle on the baking parchment and spread thinly with a palette knife to fill the circle. Sprinkle with rosemary and bake for 6–8 minutes or until tinged brown at the edges. Drape over the prepared dariole moulds. Place in the oven for 3–4 minutes. Cool for a few seconds, then release from the moulds and leave to cool.

5 For the salad, blend the basil with 5–6 tbsp oil. Pour through a sieve set over a bowl. Season the tomatoes with salt and a splash of olive oil.

6 To serve, set a basket on each plate and divide tomatoes between them. Top with a scoop of sorbet and garnish with shredded basil and oil.

Celeriac soup with curried scallops

Tim Kinnaird @ finalist

Preparation time 15 minutes   **Cooking time** 40 minutes   **Serves 4**

PREPARE AHEAD
Steps 1-2

Ingredients

50g (1¾oz) butter

salt and freshly ground black pepper

1 large leek, finely sliced

1 medium to large celeriac, approx. 600g (1lb 5oz) in weight, peeled and chopped into small cubes

1 litre (1¾ pints) chicken stock

4 large or 8 small scallops

1 tbsp good-quality curry powder

1 tbsp olive oil

Method

1 Melt the butter in a large pan over medium heat, add the leeks and a little salt and black pepper, and cook, stirring, for 8–10 minutes or until leeks are softened but not coloured. Add the celeriac, pour in the stock, and bring to the boil.

2 Cover and simmer for about 30 minutes, until the celeriac is tender. Purée the soup using a hand blender or by transferring to a food processor, dividing it into batches for a smoother result. Season to taste. Set aside.

3 Just before serving, dust each scallop with a little curry powder and season with salt and pepper. Heat the oil in a frying pan over a medium heat and quickly fry the scallops for 1–2 minutes only, turning once. Take care not to have the heat too high or the curry powder will burn and taste bitter.

4 To serve, reheat the soup and ladle into bowls, and place a scallop, or scallops, in the centre.

Fresh crab with feuille de brick biscuits

PREPARE AHEAD
Steps 1-3

Phil Vickery MBE @ **Celebrity champion**

Preparation time 40 minutes   **Cooking time** 40 minutes   **Serves 4**

Ingredients

For the crab

2 white onions, chopped

2 carrots, chopped

2 celery sticks, chopped

2 garlic cloves, halved

2 sprigs of thyme

2 bay leaves

2 large crabs

2 red chillies, finely chopped

100g (3½oz) spring onions, finely chopped

2 red onions, finely chopped

2 tbsp finely chopped coriander

2 tbsp finely chopped basil

1 tbsp finely snipped chives

1 garlic clove, finely chopped

zest of 2 lemons

dash of fish sauce

dash of sesame oil

For the biscuits

4 sheets of feuille de brick pastry

25g (scant 1oz) butter, melted

12 basil leaves

1 tbsp freshly ground red or pink peppercorns

1 tbsp white sesame seeds

1 tbsp black sesame seeds

For the herb dressing

100ml (3½fl oz) vegetable oil

1 bunch of basil

1 tbsp snipped chives

1 garlic clove, chopped

salt and freshly ground black pepper

For the crabmeat dressing

reserved brown crabmeat

vegetable oil

Tabasco sauce, to taste

To serve

2 thin slices smoked pancetta

1 tbsp olive oil

handful each of micro coriander, micro basil, micro red chard, and red shiso

Method

1 To cook the crab, simmer the vegetables, garlic, thyme, and bay leaves in a large pan of water for 10 minutes. Turn up the heat, add the crabs, and boil for 20 minutes. Remove crabs and cool under the cold tap. Take the meat from the shells. Mix the white meat with remaining ingredients and set aside. Reserve the brown meat.

2 For the biscuits, preheat the oven to 180°C (350°F/Gas 4). Cut pastry into twenty-four 6cm (2½in) squares, and brush with butter. Put 12 on a baking tray lined with baking parchment. Place a basil leaf on top of each, sprinkle with pepper, put a second square on top.and sprinkle with the sesame seeds. Cover with a sheet of baking parchment, followed by a baking tray and press it down. Bake in the oven for 6–8 minutes, or until golden brown. Set aside.

TECHNIQUE

How to deshell a cooked crab

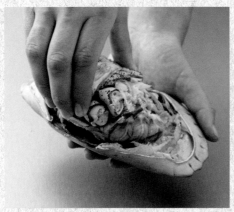

1 Pull away claws and legs and set aside. Twist off the tail flap and discard. To separate body from the carapace, crack it under the tail, then prise apart the two sections pulling the body from tail end.

2 Remove the gills (dead man's fingers) attached to the main body, and check for stray gills left in the carapace. Remove stomach sac as well, which will either be attached to the body or in the carapace.

3 For the herb dressing, blitz the ingredients in a food processor until smooth. For the crab dressing, mix the brown crabmeat with some vegetable oil to loosen and add Tabasco sauce and season to taste. Set aside.

4 Just before serving, fry the pancetta in the oil until crisp. Drain and crumble into small pieces. Using a 5cm (2in) chef's ring, place 3 mounds of the crab on each plate, spoon a line of crab dressing on top, and 3 lines of herb dressing on the plate. Rest a biscuit on each mound, and scatter micro leaves and pancetta around.

3 Cut the body of the crab into quarters and pick out the white meat, using a seafood fork or lobster pick. Remove any shell or membrane. Scoop out the brown meat from the carapace with a spoon.

4 Break shell of the claws with a lobster or nut cracker. Extract meat, and remove the cartilage. Remove any membrane or shell. Crack legs across their narrowest part, then pick out the meat with a fork.

Pavé of salmon, vegetable terrine, tomato consommé, and quail's egg jelly

Adam Fargin @ Professionals quarter-finalist

Preparation time 45 minutes   **Cooking time** 15 minutes   **Serves 4**

PREPARE AHEAD
Steps 1-4

Ingredients

8 quail's eggs

2 tbsp olive oil

450–500g (1lb–1lb 2oz) centre-cut fillet of salmon, skin on

125g (4½oz) samphire (or fine asparagus)

25g (scant 1oz) unsalted butter

sea salt

white peppercorns

For the consommé

1 kg (2¼lb) San Marzano or vine-ripened tomatoes

8–10 basil stalks

8 small or 4 long gelatine sheets, soaked

For the vegetable terrine

2 courgettes, 1 sliced lengthways, the other into discs

1 large purple aubergine, sliced lengthways

2 red peppers, deseeded and sliced

1 yellow pepper, deseeded and sliced

100g (3½oz) baby carrots, stalks on

35g (1¼oz) basil leaves

Method

1 Blanch the quail's eggs in boiling water for 2 minutes. Refresh in cold water and, once cold, peel under cold water and set aside. To make the consommé, whizz the tomatoes and basil stalks to a pulp in a blender. Season and place pulp in a jelly bag over a bowl. Leave overnight in the fridge to drain. Heat the liquid collected until slightly hot, whisk in the gelatine leaves, and leave to cool. Reserve 100ml (3½fl oz) consommé for the vegetable terrine.

2 Line a 600ml (1 pint) terrine mould or loaf tin with cling film, fill with half the remaining consommé and freeze for 30–40 minutes. When semi-hard, put in the quail's eggs and fill to the top with the remaining consommé. Return to the fridge until set – about 1½ hours.

3 In a frying pan, heat the oil to 55°C (131°F). Add the salmon, cover, and keep temperature constant for 14 minutes, then remove salmon and allow to cool for 30 minutes. Refrigerate.

4 For the vegetable terrine, chargrill the lengthways-cut courgette, aubergine, and half the peppers. Place the courgette discs, remaining peppers, and carrots in a pan of salted boiling water until cooked – about 10 minutes. Drain and refresh in iced water. Line a 1.2 litre (2 pint) loaf tin or terrine with cling film, add the chargrilled aubergine and courgette. Fill the centre with the boiled vegetables and basil and top with the chargrilled peppers. Pour reserved tomato consommé over. Refrigerate until set.

5 To serve, let the salmon to come to room temperature. Cut into 4. Sauté the samphire in the butter for 2–3 minutes, then season. Cut the jellied terrine through the eggs, and put a slice on 4 plates, with a slice of vegetable terrine and a piece of salmon, topped with samphire.

Garlic soup with scallop tartare, croûtes, and pancetta

PREPARE AHEAD
Steps 1-4

Gillian Wylie Ⓜ quarter-finalist
Preparation time 10 minutes   **Cooking time** 30 minutes   **Serves 4**

Ingredients

10 garlic cloves

1 medium potato, peeled and cubed

1 litre (1¾ pints) chicken stock or vegetable stock

about 4 tbsp double cream

salt and white pepper

For the croûtes

1 short, skinny baguette

4 slices of pancetta

For the tartare

4 scallops, without coral, diced

a few chives, finely snipped

drizzle of extra virgin olive oil

Method

1 In a large pan, cover the garlic cloves with water and bring to the boil; drain and discard the water. Repeat this sequence three times to mellow the flavour of the garlic.

2 Add the potato and stock to the garlic and simmer for about 20 minutes until the potato is very soft. Blitz with a hand blender, or transfer to a food processor and blend until smooth. Add a little of the cream to taste – too much will start to dilute the flavour rather than enhance it. Season with salt and pepper and set aside.

3 For the croûtes, heat grill to high. Cut 2 thin slices on the diagonal from the baguette. Toast on both sides, then cut each slice through the middle and toast the cut sides. Set aside.

4 Grill the pancetta on both sides until crispy. Set aside.

5 To serve, reheat the soup and ladle into 4 bowls. Place a diced scallop in the centre of each bowl – the heat of the soup will cook it. Lay a toasted croûte and a slice of pancetta on top, sprinkle with chives, and dress with a drizzle of olive oil.

Spinach and ricotta ravioli with walnut pesto, and a cream and basil sauce

Chris Gates @ finalist

Preparation time 1 hour 20 minutes   **Cooking time** 10 minutes   **Serves 4**

PREPARE AHEAD
Steps 1-5

Ingredients

For the pasta
150g (5½oz) "00" pasta flour, plus extra to dust

350g (12oz) semolina flour

2 large eggs

10 egg yolks

For the filling
20g (¾oz) butter

200g (7oz) spinach

salt and freshly ground black pepper

350g (12oz) ricotta or soft goat's cheese

grated zest of 1 lemon

For the pesto
30g (1oz) walnuts

1 garlic clove, chopped

1 bunch of basil

25g (scant 1oz) Parmesan cheese, freshly grated

olive oil

For the sauce
1 shallot, finely chopped

1 tbsp olive oil

500ml (16fl oz) double cream

juice of 1 lemon

Method

1 To make the pasta, blitz all the ingredients in a food processor until the mixture is like breadcrumbs. Empty onto a floured surface and knead into a silky dough. Wrap in cling film and leave to rest in the fridge for about 1 hour.

2 Meanwhile, make the filling. Melt the butter in a large pan, add the spinach and cook over a low heat until it wilts. Remove from the

heat and season with salt and pepper. Squeeze out any water and place in a bowl. Add the ricotta and lemon zest and season to taste.

3 For the pesto, toast the walnuts in a dry pan until golden. Using a pestle and mortar, break them up with the garlic and basil leaves, reserving the stalks and a few leaves to garnish. Add the Parmesan, loosen with oil, and season.

4 For the cream sauce, sauté the chopped shallot in a pan with the oil until softened. Add the reserved basil stalks and soften for 3–4 minutes. Add the cream and allow to reduce slightly. Season with salt and pepper and add the lemon juice.

TECHNIQUE

How to use a pasta machine

1 Flatten the pasta dough into a circle and pass through the pasta machine on the thickest setting 3 times. This will make the dough spread out to fill the full width of the machine.

2 Fold the pasta dough into thirds, then flatten it , and pass through the machine again. Repeat this process 6 times (lightly dusting the dough with flour once or twice to prevent it sticking).

5 Using a pasta machine, roll out the pasta to the thinnest setting. Make 2 rectangular dough sheets. Place teaspoons of the filling on top of the first dough sheet, about 5cm (2in) apart. Brush round the heaps of filling with a little water and top with the second sheet of dough. Using your fingers, press round the filling to remove any air. Cut out the ravioli, using a fluted pastry cutter about 5cm (2in) in diameter. Set aside.

6 To serve, cook the ravioli in boiling salted water for about 5 minutes. Drain and serve on warm plates with the reheated cream sauce and some pesto spooned over, garnished with a scattering of basil leaves.

3 Continue to roll the pasta through the machine, decreasing the thickness setting each time. Turn the handle with one hand and support tdough with the other, as it gradually becomes thinner.

4 To save time, press the edges of the pasta sheet together to create a loop. This will avoid the need to keep removing the dough from the machine and feeding it back in.

Gnocchi with blue cheese, Greek yogurt, and pine nut sauce

inspired by **Midge Ure** @ Celebrity finalist

Preparation time 30 minutes   **Cooking time** 40 minutes   **Serves 4**

PREPARE AHEAD
Steps 1-4

Ingredients

500g (1lb 2oz) floury potatoes, left whole and unpeeled

salt and freshly ground black pepper

1 egg

150g (5½oz) "00" pasta flour

rocket, to serve

For the sauce

250ml (8fl oz) white wine

125g (4½oz) Dolcelatte cheese, chopped

3 tbsp Greek yogurt

1 tsp clear honey

60g (2oz) pine nuts, toasted

Method →

Method

1 To make the gnocchi, place the potatoes in a large pan of cold water, add a sprinkling of salt and bring to the boil for 25–30 minutes, or until the potatoes are cooked all the way through. Don't be tempted to peel and chop them to speed this up – the skins help to prevent the potatoes taking on any water and making the mixture too soggy. Once they are cooked, drain and allow to cool slightly, then peel with a knife.

2 Pass the potatoes through a potato ricer and then press through a sieve. Season with salt and beat in the egg. Add half of the flour and mix in well until smooth, then tip out onto a lightly floured surface and incorporate the remaining flour while kneading the mixture into a dough. Form into long cylindrical rolls (see below) and cut crossways into 3cm (1¼in) pieces.

TECHNIQUE

How to shape gnocchi

1 Mix gnochi dough according to your recipe. Take a piece and lightly roll back and forth on a floured surface to form a long roll, as thick as your forefinger. Repeat with the remaining dough.

2 Cut the rolled-out cylinders of dough into 3cm (1¼in) pieces, shape into crescents, and press onto the back of a fork to make indentations. Place on a floured tray until ready to cook.

3 Place the finished gnocchi on a floured tray, ensuring that they do not touch each other or they will stick together. Cover with cling film and set aside.

4 To make the sauce, bring the wine to the boil in a saucepan, lower the heat and leave the wine to reduce by about a third. Stir in the Dolcelatte cheese until melted, and then the yogurt, honey, and some seasoning. Finally, add two-thirds of the toasted pine nuts.

5 Just before serving, bring a large pan of salted water to the boil and slide the gnocchi into the water from the tray. Cook for 2 minutes, or until the gnocchi start to float to the surface, then drain well.

6 Divide the gnocchi between 4 warm serving plates. Reheat the sauce and pour over the gnocchi. Sprinkle over the remaining pine nuts and some rocket leaves, and serve.

Stuffed saddle of suckling pig with a crispy pig's ear salad

Tom Whitaker @ finalist

Preparation time 2 hours 30 minutes   **Cooking time** 3 hours   **Serves 6**

PREPARE AHEAD
Steps 1-10

Ingredients

For the broth

250ml (8fl oz) dry white wine

2 litres (3½ pints) ham stock

2 bay leaves

3 pig's ears

4 pig's trotters

2 ham hocks

For the crubeens

reserved trotter meat, shredded

reserved ham hock meat, shredded

1 tbsp finely chopped thyme

1 tbsp finely chopped parsley

1 tbsp English mustard powder

salt and freshly ground black pepper

200g (7oz) plain flour

2 eggs, beaten

200g (7oz) panko breadcrumbs

vegetable oil, for deep frying

For the stuffing

200g (7oz) pig's liver, finely chopped

200g (7oz) Bury black pudding, finely chopped

5 pickled walnuts, crushed

2 tbsp finely chopped thyme

2 tbsp finely chopped parsley

25g (scant 1oz) rolled oats

1 tsp mustard seeds

For the suckling pig

1 tbsp fennel seeds

1 boned saddle of suckling pig

2 tbsp olive oil

Ingredients

For the salad

200ml (7fl oz) malt vinegar

3 tbsp sherry vinegar

50g (1¾oz) caster sugar

2 tsp fennel seeds

2 tsp coriander seeds

1 bay leaf

3 celery sticks, finely sliced

3 shallots, finely sliced

reserved pig's ears

100g (3½oz) plain flour

vegetable oil, for deep frying

leaves from 1 head of celery

1 head of chicory, leaves separated

20 sorrel leaves

2 tbsp chopped parsley

juice of ½ lemon

2 tbsp olive oil

For the pomme purée

6 King Edward potatoes, peeled and halved

500ml (16fl oz) whole milk

200ml (7fl oz) double cream

2 bay leaves

salt and white pepper

few drops of hickory essence

For the sauce

reserved ham broth

1 tbsp honey

To garnish

6 sprigs of thyme

Method

1 First make the broth. Pour the white wine into an open pressure cooker pan, bring to the boil and reduce by half. Add the ham stock, bay leaves, pig's ears and trotters, and ham hocks. Seal the pressure cooker and cook on low heat for 1¼ hours. Remove the meat and set the ears aside, then strain the broth through a fine sieve into a clean pan and set aside. Strip the meat and fat from the hock and trotters, taking as much soft fat as you can as this gives texture and flavour. Discard any leftover skin and cartilage and mix the meat and fat thoroughly in a bowl.

2 For the crubeens, mix the shredded trotter and hock meat with the thyme, parsley, and mustard powder, then season to taste with salt and pepper. Press into a non-stick baking tin to a depth of 3cm (1¼in), then cover the surface with cling film. Chill for 30–45 minutes in the fridge until set. Once set, cut into even squares of about 3cm (1¼in). Dip each cube in the flour and shake off any excess, then dip in the beaten eggs, and finally the panko breadcrumbs, ensuring each cube is evenly coated. Set aside.

3 To make the stuffing, place all the ingredients in a large bowl and mix thoroughly until you have an even consistency – roughly that of sausage meat. Season with salt and pepper.

4 To cook the suckling pig, preheat the oven to 130°C (250°F/ Gas ½). Toast the fennel seeds in a dry frying pan until fragrant, then crush in a pestle and mortar with salt and pepper. With a sharp knife, score lines widthways across the skin of the saddle, about 5mm (¼in) apart, and rub the toasted fennel seed mixture into the skin.

5 Mould the stuffing into a sausage shape and place down the centre of the saddle. Fold the skin flaps into the centre (trim off excess if they overlap) and then sow up the belly with a larding needle and thread.

6 Heat the olive oil in a frying pan and sear the saddle until browned on all sides, then transfer to a roasting tin. Roast for 50 minutes to 1 hour, then remove from the oven and turn the oven up to its highest temperature. Return the saddle to the oven for 10 minutes or until the skin is crisp. Remove from the oven and leave to rest for at least 30 minutes.

7 Meanwhile, to make the pickles for the salad, combine the vinegars, sugar, and spices in a saucepan. Bring to the boil, simmer for 20 minutes, then strain into a bowl. Add the celery and shallots to the strained liquid, then leave for 30 minutes until soft. Drain and set aside to cool.

8 Prepare the pomme purée by putting the potatoes in a pan with the milk, cream, and bay leaves and simmer until tender. Remove the bay leaves and discard. Drain the potatoes, reserving the cooking liquid, and transfer to a food processor along with a little of the cooking liquid. With the motor running, keep adding a little cooking liquid until you have a smooth,

TECHNIQUE

How to mash potatoes

1 Boil the potatoes until they are tender. Drain through a colander, then return them to the pan. Add butter, cream, salt, pepper, and nutmeg to taste. Re-cover the pan and leave for 5 minutes.

2 Using a potato masher, mash the potatoes until they are smooth and fluffy. Adjust the seasoning and add extra butter and cream, if desired. Keep hot until ready to serve.

thick purée. Pass through a fine sieve and season
to taste with salt and white pepper. Stir in a few
drops of hickory essence. Set aside.

9 Preheat the oven to 180°C (350°F/Gas 4).
Scatter the thyme sprigs for the garnish
over the bottom of a small roasting tray and
roast for 8–10 minutes until crisp, taking care
not to burn them. Set aside.

10 To make the sauce, bring the ham broth
to the boil, add the honey, and reduce
until syrupy. Season to taste and set aside.

11 Just before serving, deep fry the crubeens
in vegetable oil for 3 minutes until golden
and crisp, then drain on kitchen paper. Slice
the reserved pigs ears finely, and roll in seasoned
flour. Deep fry at 180°C (350°F) for 3 minutes or
until crisp, then drain on kitchen paper.

12 Mix the pickled celery and shallots for
the salad with the celery, chicory and
sorrel leaves, and parsley in a bowl and toss
to combine. Add the crisp pig's ears and dress
the salad with the lemon juice, olive oil, and
salt and pepper to taste.

To serve: Reheat the pomme purée and place in
a piping bag. Pipe onto either plates or wooden
serving boards. Carve the roasted saddle into
thick slices and arrange 3 on each plate or board
with 3 crubeens and a small helping of the
salad. Garnish with the roasted thyme and
serve with hot sauce in a small jug alongside.

White chocolate mousse millefeuilles with raspberry and elderflower jellies

Claire Lara @ Professionals champion

Preparation time 1 hour   **Cooking time** 30 minutes   **Serves 4**

> PREPARE AHEAD
> Steps 1-5

Ingredients

5 leaves of gelatine

200ml (7fl oz) double cream

150g (5½oz) Valrhona white chocolate

400g (14oz) raspberries

150g (5½oz) caster sugar, plus extra for scattering over the filo sheets

3 tbsp elderflower cordial

4 sheets of filo pastry

50g (1¾oz) butter, melted

2 tsp chopped freeze-dried raspberries

Method

1 Soak 2 of the leaves of gelatine in cold water for at least 10 minutes to soften. Whip the cream until soft peaks form.

2 Melt the chocolate in a bowl set over a pan of simmering water, making sure the bowl is clear of the water. Remove from the heat and, while chocolate is still warm (not hot), squeeze excess water from the gelatine and stir it into the chocolate. Whisk mixture into the whipped cream and transfer to a piping bag with a plain nozzle. Place in the fridge for 20 minutes to set.

3 Meanwhile, place the remaining gelatine in cold water to soften. Reserving 12 raspberries, whizz the rest to a purée with the sugar in a food processor, then pass through a sieve.

4 Place the raspberry purée and elderflower cordial in a pan and heat gently, then stir in the gelatine. Warm over low heat until the gelatine is dissolved. Pour into 12 mini muffin tins, sit a raspberry on top of each and put in the fridge to set.

5 Preheat the oven to 200°C (400°F/Gas 6). Cut each sheet of filo pastry into 4 rectangles. Brush with melted butter and sugar and bake in the oven for 3 minutes until crispy, then remove and cool. Scatter with freeze-dried raspberries. Set aside.

6 To serve, on each plate pipe 3–4 lines of mousse on top of a filo rectangle and top with another piece of filo. Repeat twice, finishing with a piece of filo pastry. Serve with the jellies alongside.

How to use gelatine leaves

1 Place the required number of leaves of gelatine in enough cold water, or other liquid, to cover them fully for at least 10 minutes. Squeeze out as much of the water as possible before using.

2 In a saucepan, warm some water or whatever liquid is specified in your chosen recipe. Add the gelatine, and stir to dissolve completely before leaving the solution to cool.

Floating islands with mango

Neil Mackenzie @ Professionals quarter-finalist

Preparation time 40 minutes   **Cooking time** 15 minutes   **Serves 4**

PREPARE AHEAD
Steps 1-5

Ingredients

4 eggs, separated

130g (4½oz) sugar

¼tsp cream of tartar

250ml (8fl oz) milk

250ml (8fl oz) double cream

1 vanilla pod, split, seeds scraped out and reserved

2 Alphonso mangoes, peeled and roughly diced

juice of 1 lime

Method

1 Make meringue by whisking 2 of the egg whites until stiff. Gradually add 100g (3½oz) sugar and the cream of tartar, whisking as you do so. Whisk until the mixture is glossy and stiff.

2 In a shallow pan, heat the milk and cream with the scraped out vanilla pod until just warm.

3 Use 2 large spoons to shape meringue into 8 quenelles. Add to the milk and cream mixture and poach them gently for 5 minutes. Meanwhile, line a tray with cling film. Remove the meringues from the pan, transfer them to the tray, and place in the fridge. Strain the milk mixture through a sieve.

4 Make crème anglaise by whisking the egg yolks with the vanilla seeds and 30g (1oz) sugar. Pour in the milk mixture. Transfer to a pan and cook over low heat, stirring, until thickened and the mixture coats the back of a spoon. Cool and then chill in the fridge.

5 Place the diced mango in a bowl and add the lime juice and a little sugar to sweeten, if desired. Set aside.

6 To serve, take 4 clean glasses and place some mango in the bottom of each. Spoon on the chilled crème anglaise. Apply a blow torch to the meringues and place on top.

White chocolate tower with dark chocolate mousse

Cheryl Avery @ quarter-finalist
Preparation time 1 hour   **Serves 4**

PREPARE AHEAD
Steps 1-5

Ingredients

150g (5½oz) raspberries

1–2 tbsp Kirsch

200g (7oz) white chocolate

4 sprigs of mint leaves, to decorate

For the dark chocolate mousse

125g (4½oz) caster sugar

2 large eggs, whites only

250g (9oz) dark chocolate (70% cocoa), broken into pieces

150ml (5fl oz) double cream

60ml (2fl oz) kirsch

Method

1 Make an Italian meringue base for the mousse by placing 60ml (2fl oz) water with the caster sugar and in a heavy saucepan. Bring to the boil and then simmer gently for about 5 minutes or until the mixture is pale, thick, and syrupy.

2 Whisk the egg whites with an electric mixer until stiff. Then, with the machine still running, gradually add the hot sugar syrup in a thin stream and continue to whisk until the meringue is cold. Cover and place in the fridge.

3 Put the raspberries in a small bowl, sprinkle with the kirsch, and set aside.

4 To make the chocolate mousse, melt the dark chocolate in a heatproof bowl placed over a pan of simmering water. Meanwhile, lightly whip the cream in a large bowl until it forms soft peaks. Fold in the melted chocolate, kirsch, and the prepared Italian meringue. Cover and chill in the fridge for 10 minutes.

5 Melt the white chocolate in a bowl placed over a pan of simmering water. Pour the melted chocolate over a slab of marble or some baking parchment, spread out to produce a thin sheet, and leave to set. Dip a 9cm (3½in) round cutter in hot water and use it to cut out 12 discs of white chocolate.

TECHNIQUE

How to whip egg whites

1 Place the egg whites in a metal or ceramic bowl that is clean, free of any traces of grease, and completely dry. Begin whisking them slowly, using a small range of motion.

2 Continue whisking steadily, using larger strokes, until the whites lose their translucency and start to foam. The aim is to incorporate as much air as possible so the whites increase in volume.

6 To assemble, fill a piping bag with the chilled dark chocolate mousse mixture. Place a white chocolate disc on each serving plate and pipe a layer of chocolate mousse on top. Add a layer of the kirsch-soaked raspberries. Repeat, then top the tower with a final disc of white chocolate. Top with more raspberries and a sprig of mint leaves. Spoon a few more kirsch-soaked raspberries alongside the tower and serve.

3 Continue whisking, increasing your speed and range of motion until the whites have expanded to the desired degree and are stiff, but not dry.

4 Test by lifting the whisk away: the peaks should be firm and glossy, and the tips should hang. Take care not to overwhisk, or the air bubbles that have formed will collapse.

Mango parfait with a passion fruit glaze and lime and vodka sorbet

Sara Danesin Medio @ finalist

Preparation time 1 hour   **Cooking time** 10–30 minutes   **Serves 6**

PREPARE AHEAD
Steps 1-5

Ingredients

For the lime sorbet

250ml (8fl oz) water

225g (8oz) sugar

200ml (7fl oz) fresh lime juice

1 tsp grated lime zest

75ml (2½fl oz) vodka

For the parfait

3 large egg yolks

75g (2½oz) caster sugar

250g (9oz) Alphonso mango purée

175g (6oz) double cream

For the glaze

2 gelatine leaves

5 fresh passion fruit, split

20g (¾oz) caster sugar

To serve

1 large, ripe Alphonso mango, thinly sliced, and with six 6cm (2½in) squares cut

6 sprigs of micro red amaranth

3 vanilla pods, halved and split

Method

1 First make the sorbet. Heat the water and sugar in a saucepan until the sugar has dissolved. Transfer to a jug and combine with the lime juice and zest and vodka. Leave to cool, then pour into an ice-cream machine and churn until set. Transfer to a plastic container with a lid and store in the freezer until ready to serve. Alternatively, place the mixture in a freezerproof container and freeze until mushy. Whisk until the ice crystals are broken up. Return to the freezer and repeat the process twice.

2 Next, make the parfait. Wrap cling film around the bases of six 6cm (2½in) square metal mousse moulds, each 3cm (1¼in) deep, to create a tight seal. Place moulds on a baking tray.

3 Place the egg yolks and sugar in a heatproof bowl and beat lightly to mix. Set the bowl over a pan of lightly simmering water, making sure the base does not touch the water. Whisk the mixture until it triples in volume and is thick and pale. When you lift the beaters, the mixture should be thick enough to leave a ribbon trail across the surface. Fold in the mango purée.

4 In a separate bowl, whip the cream to soft peaks, then fold carefully into the mango mixture. Divide the mixture between the prepared mousse moulds and transfer to the freezer for 2 hours or until firm.

5 Prepare the glaze by soaking the gelatine in cold water for 10 minutes, or until soft. Scrape out the passion fruit and place the seeds and juice in a small pan with the sugar. Gently heat to a simmer, then remove from the heat. Drain the gelatine, squeezing out any excess water, then whisk into the passion fruit until dissolved. Transfer to a bowl and refrigerate for 1 hour, until almost set. Spoon over the set parfaits in the moulds. Chill to set.

6 To serve, lay a mango square in 6 small dishes and top with a quenelle of sorbet and a sprig of amaranth. Place the dishes of sorbet on 6 larger plates. Unmould a parfaits onto each plate alongside the dish of sorbet. Decorate the parfaits with a slice of mango and some split vanilla pod.

Pineapple carpaccio with mascarpone and date mousse, and kiwi coulis

Renaud Marin @ Professionals quarter-finalist

Preparation time 30 minutes   **Cooking time** 20 minutes   **Serves 4**

<table>
<tr><td>PREPARE AHEAD
Steps 1-5</td></tr>
</table>

Ingredients

250ml (8fl oz) mineral water

110g (3¾oz) caster sugar

10g (¼oz) whole allspice

1 clove

½ cinnamon stick

½ pineapple, peeled and cored

125g (4½oz) mascarpone cheese

2 tbsp whipping cream

50g (1¾oz) pitted Medjool dates

3 kiwis, peeled and roughly chopped

Method

1 Put the water, 50g (1¾oz) of sugar, and all the spices into a pan and slowly bring to the boil. Once the sugar has dissolved, increase the heat and leave to boil for 15 minutes.

2 Finely slice the pineapple with a mandoline or a sharp knife. Pour the syrup over the pineapple slices in a large tray. Cool in the fridge.

3 For the mousse, whip the cheese, cream, and 50g (1¾oz) of the sugar until smooth.

4 Finely dice the dates and add to the mousse and whip again until the mix is even. Leave to set and rest in the fridge.

5 To make the coulis, put the kiwi pieces in a blender with the remaining sugar and mix until smooth. Pass through a fine sieve into a clean bowl. Set aside.

6 To serve, drain the pineapple slices and arrange on 4 plates. Drizzle over some kiwi coulis and add a quenelle of the mousse in the middle.

Liquorice-poached pears, and sablé biscuits with milk and honey ice cream

Tom Whitaker @ finalist

Preparation time 1 hour 15 minutes   **Cooking time** 30 minutes   **Serves 4**

PREPARE AHEAD
Steps 1-11

Ingredients

For the ice cream
600ml (1 pint) whole milk

2 tbsp clear honey

1½ tsp liquid glucose

5 tbsp condensed milk

4 tbsp double cream

For the praline
100g (3½oz) caster sugar

25g (scant 1oz) toasted, flaked almonds

For the mint leaves
12 large mint leaves

1 egg white

caster sugar

For the poached pears
300g (10oz) caster sugar

1 liquorice stick

2 tsp liquorice essence

4 tsp crème de cassis

2 Williams pears

For the sablé biscuits
30g (1oz) icing sugar, plus extra for dusting

125g (4½oz) unsalted butter, cubed

1 vanilla pod, seeds only

125g (4½oz) plain flour

For the brandy cream
120ml (4fl oz) double cream

1 tsp icing sugar

4 tsp reserved poaching syrup reduction

1 tsp brandy

To serve
4 tsp reserved poaching syrup reduction

1 tsp brandy

Method

Method

1 Make the milk and honey ice cream. Put the milk and honey into a pan, bring to the boil, and reduce by half. Strain into a jug and leave to cool. When cooled, whisk in the glucose, condensed milk, and double cream.

2 Pour the mixture into an ice-cream machine and churn until set. Transfer to a plastic container with a lid and store in the freezer until serving. Alternatively, pour the mixture into a freezerproof container and freeze until mushy. Whisk until the ice crystals are broken up. Return to the freezer and repeat the process twice.

3 Meanwhile, make the praline. Line a baking tray with baking parchment. Put the sugar into a wide pan and heat, without stirring, until it caramelizes and turns a deep golden brown, about 140–150°C (275–300°F) on a sugar thermometer. Remove from the heat and add the flaked almonds.

4 Pour the mixture on to the prepared baking tray and spread out with a spatula. Allow to cool until hard and brittle, then break into smaller pieces and place in a food processor. Blitz until crumbly.

5 Meanwhile, prepare the crystallized mint leaves. Wash the leaves and pat dry on kitchen paper. Beat the egg white lightly with a fork on a plate and dip the leaves in it. Drain off excess egg white and sprinkle leaves liberally with caster sugar. Place on baking parchment on a baking tray and leave to dry in a warm place.

6 Make the poaching syrup for the pears. Put 50g (1¾oz) of the sugar in a pan and melt on high heat until it is a rich, dark caramel. Do not stir. Add 500ml (16fl oz) hot water (take care, it may splutter), the remaining 250g (9oz) sugar, the liquorice stick, liquorice essence, and crème de cassis. Stir until dissolved, then leave to infuse for 20 minutes.

7 Bring the syrup back to the boil, then peel, core and halve the pears and add to syrup. Remove immediately from the heat, cover, and leave to infuse for 15–20 minutes until translucent. Remove the pears with a slotted spoon. Set aside to cool.

8 Pour half of the poaching liquid into a separate pan and reduce until syrupy. Set the poaching syrup reduction aside to cool.

9 Meanwhile, make the sablé biscuits. Sift the icing sugar into a bowl, add the butter and vanilla seeds, and stir to combine. Sift in the flour and rub in with the fingertips to form a smooth dough. Using a large sheet of cling film, roll the dough into a log shape and chill in the fridge until it is firm.

10 Preheat the oven to 180°C (350°F/Gas 4). Slice the dough into 5mm (¼in) thick rounds and place well apart on a baking tray lined with baking parchment. Bake for 10–12 minutes until pale gold in colour. Dust with icing sugar. Transfer to a wire rack to cool.

11 Whisk the brandy cream ingredients until the mixture forms soft peaks. Chill.

To serve: Arrange 3 frosted mint leaves in a three-cornered star on each of 4 serving plates. Quickly coat 4 scoops of the ice cream in the praline crumbs and place in the centre of the mint leaves. Add a poached pear half to one side of each plate. Mix the poaching syrup reduction with the brandy and spoon a little in each pear cavity. Top each pear with a quenelle of the brandy cream. Lay a sablé biscuit to one side of the each pear and serve immediately.

Lavender mousse with honeycomb and a blackberry sauce

Mat Follas @ champion

Preparation time 50 minutes   **Serves 4**

PREPARE AHEAD
Steps 1-6

Ingredients

For the blackberry sauce

300g (10oz) blackberries

200g (7oz) caster sugar

For the lavender mousse

15g (½oz) gelatine leaves, cut into pieces

500ml (16fl oz) whole milk

5 egg yolks

40g (1¼oz) caster sugar

500ml (16fl oz) whipping cream

20g (¾oz) lavender flower heads

12 drops lavender essence

For the honeycomb

75g (2½oz) caster sugar

2 tbsp golden syrup

1 tsp bicarbonate of soda

Method

1 Set aside 12 blackberries of different sizes for decoration. Then put the remaining blackberries in a pan with the sugar and add 100ml (3½fl oz) cold water, stir and heat gently until the sugar has dissolved. Bring the sauce to the boil, reduce the heat, and simmer for 5 minutes or until the sauce has reduced by half and thickened. Pass through a sieve, discard the blackberry pulp, and leave to cool.

2 Transfer the sauce into a jug and pour a little into 4 freezerproof glasses, which the mousse will be served in. Put the glasses in the freezer and set the rest of the sauce aside in the refrigerator.

3 For the lavender mousse, put the gelatine in iced water for about 10 minutes to soften. Pour the milk into a saucepan and bring it to the boil. Place the egg yolks and sugar into a bowl and mix. Stir in the hot milk. Return to the pan, stirring and warming gently for 5 minutes or until the sauce coats the back of a spoon. Drain any excess water from the gelatine and add to the pan and stir until dissolved. Set aside to cool.

4 Whip the cream until stiff peaks are formed. Add the lavender heads and combine. Stir in the lavender essence, a drop at a time, until the flavour is to your taste. Gently fold the cream into the cooled mouse mixture.

5 Remove the glasses from the freezer and pour the mousse mixture over the frozen berry sauce. Return to the freezer for 20 minutes, then place in the fridge.

6 To make the honeycomb, heat the sugar and golden syrup slowly in a saucepan, stirring constantly for 3 minutes or until the sugar is dissolved. Stir in the bicarbonate of soda and then pour onto a silicone sheet and leave to cool. Put into a plastic bag and gently smash it. Set aside.

7 To serve, make a line of blackberry sauce on each plate and top with 3 reserved blackberries. Add the frozen mousses and put a piece of broken honeycomb in the top of each one. Add a small pile of honeycomb crumbs alongside.

Rose-scented rice pudding with raspberry coulis and pistachios

Cassandra Williams @ quarter-finalist

Preparation time 45 minutes   **Cooking time** 40 minutes   **Serves 4**

PREPARE AHEAD
Steps 1-3

Ingredients

500ml (16fl oz) whole milk

2 tbsp caster sugar

grated zest of 1 orange

pinch of salt

85g (3oz) short-grain rice

120ml (4fl oz) double cream, whipped

1 tsp rosewater

60g (2oz) pistachio nuts, shelled and finely chopped

100g (3½oz) raspberries

For the raspberry coulis

100g (3½oz) raspberries

30g (1oz) icing sugar

juice of ½ lemon

Method

1 Put the milk, sugar, orange zest, and salt in a saucepan and bring to the boil. Add the rice and cook on low heat for 30 minutes, stirring occasionally, until the rice is soft and the liquid absorbed.

2 Remove the pan from the heat and allow the rice to cool before stirring in the whipped cream and rosewater. Spoon into four 120ml (4fl oz) pudding moulds and place in the fridge for at least 2 hours, or until set.

3 To make the raspberry coulis, blend the raspberries with the icing sugar and lemon juice in a food processor. Pass through a sieve. Set aside.

4 To serve, remove the rice puddings from the fridge and carefully unmould. Gently sprinkle the chopped pistachio nuts onto the sides of the puddings, then place them on serving plates and top with up-turned raspberries. Drizzle the coulis around the puddings and serve immediately.

Lemon posset with fresh fruit and shortbread

Linda Lusardi @ Celebrity semi-finalist

Preparation time 15 minutes   **Cooking time** 25 minutes   **Serves 4**

PREPARE AHEAD
Steps 1-8

Ingredients

For the posset

750ml (1¼ pints) double cream

200g (7oz) caster sugar

juice of 3 lemons

For the shortbread

200g (7oz) unsalted butter, softened

60g (2oz) icing sugar

1 tsp vanilla extract

200g (7oz) plain flour

½ tsp salt

150g (5½oz) dark chocolate, broken into small pieces

To finish

250g (9oz) fresh fruit: strawberries, raspberries, and blackberries

Method →

Method

1 Preheat the oven to 180°C (350°F/Gas 4). For the posset, put the cream and sugar into a saucepan and bring to the boil. Simmer for 6 minutes, then remove from the heat. Whisk in the lemon juice, then leave to cool.

2 Divide the mixture between 4 serving glasses, then chill in the fridge for at least 2 hours, or until set.

3 Meanwhile make the shortbread. Using an electric hand whisk, cream the butter and sugar together until pale and fluffy, then stir in the vanilla extract. Sift the flour and salt into the mixture and stir until combined.

4 Wrap the dough in cling film, then chill in the fridge for 1 hour.

5 Remove the dough from the fridge, unwrap, and place on a lightly floured surface. Roll out to a thickness of 5mm (¼in), then cut out with a heart-shaped biscuit cutter. Transfer to a non-stick baking tray, then chill in the fridge for 30 minutes.

6 Bake the shortbread for 8–10 minutes in the hot oven until lightly golden, then transfer to a wire rack to cool.

7 Put the chocolate into a heatproof bowl and set it over a pan of gently simmering water. Stir until the chocolate has melted, then remove from the heat.

8 Put the chocolate in a paper piping bag with the point snipped off, or use a teaspoon, and drizzle the chocolate over the shortbread biscuits in a zigzag pattern. Leave to set.

9 When ready to serve, top the possets with the mixed fruits and serve with shortbread biscuits.

Lime posset with caramelized pineapple and basil cream

Lee Groves @ Professionals semi-finalist

Preparation time 40 minutes   **Cooking time** 20 minutes   **Serves 4–6**

PREPARE AHEAD
Steps 1-4

Ingredients

600ml (1 pint) double cream

400g (7oz) caster sugar

zest and juice of 4 limes

1 small pineapple, peeled, cored, and drained of juice

1 bunch of basil

Method

1 Put 450ml (15fl oz) of the cream, half the sugar, and the lime juice and zest into a medium saucepan. Bring to the boil, stirring to dissolve the sugar, then cook gently for 5 minutes. Pour into a clean bowl, cool, and chill.

2 Dice the pineapple into 1cm (½in) cubes. Melt remaining sugar until caramelized and golden, which will take about 10 minutes. Toss the pineapple through the caramel, then cook for 10 minutes until golden and slightly softened.

3 Whip the remaining cream until stiff. Chop the basil at the last minute and fold into the cream.

4 Put a spoonful of pineapple in the bottom of 4 serving glasses. Gently divide the chilled posset mixture between the glasses and chill.

5 To serve, put a small spoonful of pineapple mix on the posset and top with a neat quenelle of basil cream.

Exploding lemon macaroons

Tim Kinnaird @ finalist

Preparation time 55 minutes   **Cooking time** 25 minutes   **Serves 4**

PREPARE AHEAD
Steps 1-9

Ingredients

For the macaroons

175g (6oz) caster sugar

3 tbsp water

4 egg whites, near their sell-by date

175g (6oz) ground almonds

175g (6oz) icing sugar

1 tsp yellow food colouring

For the lemon curd

4 egg yolks

grated zest and juice of 6 lemons

70g (2¼oz) caster sugar

70g (2¼oz) salted butter

To serve

popping candy (optional)

Method →

Method

1 Preheat the oven to 150°C (300°F/Gas 2) and line 2–3 baking sheets with baking parchment.

2 To make the macaroons, dissolve the sugar in 3 tbsp of water over low heat for about 8 minutes, stirring occasionally. Increase the heat and allow the sugar to boil for about 10 minutes, without stirring, until it reaches 118°C (244°F) – "soft boil" temperature.

3 Whisk the egg whites in a free-standing mixer until they start to foam. Still mixing, gradually, add the sugar syrup in a steady stream until the sugar is incorporated and the egg whites form stiff peaks.

TECHNIQUE

How to separate yolks and whites

1 Break the eggshell by tapping it against the rim of a bowl. Insert your fingers into the break, and gently pry the two halves apart. Some of the white will escape into the bowl. Remove any shell that falls in.

2 Gently shift the yolk back and forth between the shell halves, allowing the white to fall into the bowl. Take care to keep the yolk intact. Place the yolk in another bowl and set aside.

4 In a separate bowl, mix together the ground almonds, icing sugar, 150g (5½oz) of the egg whites, and the food colouring. Fold into the stiff egg whites, until the mixture flows like lava.

5 Pipe 5cm (2in) circles of the mixture onto the lined baking sheets, with at least 2cm (¾in) gaps between each circle. Leave for 45 minutes for the circles to dry a little and a crust to form.

6 Bake in the hot oven for about 15 minutes. Remove from the oven to cool and then gently remove the macaroon biscuits from the paper and set aside.

7 While the macaroon biscuits are resting, make the lemon curd. Put the egg yolks, lemon zest and juice, and caster sugar into a saucepan and heat gently with half the butter for about 10 minutes until the curd thickens.

8 Strain the lemon curd into a bowl to remove the zest and whisk in the remaining butter. Chill in the fridge until the curd is firm and the macaroons are cool.

9 Sandwich pairs of macaroons with lemon curd and put them back in the fridge to chill, preferably overnight.

10 Remove the macaroons from the fridge an hour before serving. Slightly moisten them by lightly brushing them with a moistened pastry brush and sprinkle with popping candy, if using.

Finishing
Touches

Whiting quenelles in shellfish broth

Dick Strawbridge @ Celebrity finalist

Preparation time 45 minutes   **Cooking time** 55 minutes   **Serves 4–6**

PREPARE AHEAD
Steps 1-4

Ingredients

For the quenelles

15g (½oz) butter, melted

40g (1¼oz) fresh breadcrumbs

100ml (3½fl oz) milk

225g (8oz) skinned whiting fillet, roughly chopped

2 tsp lemon juice

1 egg

salt and freshly ground black pepper

freshly ground nutmeg, to taste

100ml (3½fl oz) double cream

For the broth

50g (1¾oz) butter

1 onion, chopped

1 celery stick, chopped

1 carrot, chopped

450g (1lb) raw whole prawns, peeled and roughly chopped

3 tbsp brandy

100ml (3½fl oz) dry white wine

3 ripe tomatoes, approx. 225g (8oz), chopped

1.5 litres (2¾ pints) fish stock

1 large leek, halved lengthways and sliced

1 large Maris Piper or King Edward potato, approx. 300g (10oz), diced

generous pinch of saffron

extra virgin olive oil, to serve

Method

1 For the quenelles, mix together the melted butter, breadcrumbs, and milk to make a coarse paste. Cover and chill for 30 minutes.

2 Put the chilled paste, whiting, lemon juice, and egg in a food processor with some salt, pepper, and nutmeg to taste, and whizz to form a smooth paste. With the motor running, gradually add the cream. Put into a bowl, sit this in a larger bowl of iced water, cover, and set aside to chill and firm up.

3 To make the broth, melt half the butter in a large stockpot over high heat. Add the onion, celery, and carrot and cook, stirring, for 5 minutes. Next, add the prawns and brandy and cook, stirring, for a further 2 minutes. Then add

TECHNIQUE

How to make fish stock

1 On a low heat, melt a knob of butter in a large saucepan or stockpot. Add the fish bones and stir until they smell of cooked fish, taking great care that they do not burn.

2 Add water, vegetables, and seasoning, and bring the liquid to the boil. Skim away any foam on the surface, and simmer for 30–40 minutes before straining through a fine sieve.

the white wine, tomatoes, and hot fish stock and bring just to the boil. Reduce the heat and simmer for 30 minutes.

4 Blend the broth, in batches, in a hand blender or food processor until smooth. Pass through a fine sieve into a large bowl, using the back of a soup ladle to push out as much as possible. You should end up with about 1.7 litres (3 pints) of broth. Set aside.

5 About 30 minutes before serving, place the stockpot over a medium heat. Add the remaining butter, leek, and potato and cook, stirring, for 3–4 minutes. Add the saffron and the prepared 1.7 litres (3 pints) of broth and bring just to the boil. Reduce the heat so the mixture is barely simmering. Season to taste.

6 For each quenelle, scoop a generous spoonful of the fish mixture onto a dessert spoon. Then, with a second, equal-sized spoon, shape the mixture into a rugby-ball shape, moving it from one spoon to the other. Repeat to make 4–6 quenelles. Lower quenelles into the simmering broth, and poach for 5 minutes, turning halfway. Divide between 4–6 warmed serving bowls and spoon the broth all around them. Drizzle with extra virgin olive oil to serve.

Glazed goat's cheese and beetroot with pea shoots salad

Wendi Peters @ Celebrity finalist

Preparation time 45 minutes   **Cooking time** 30 minutes   **Serves 4**

PREPARE AHEAD
Steps 1-5

Ingredients

3 large beetroots

10 raw baby beets

3 sprigs of thyme, plus 2 tbsp leaves

4 individual goat's cheeses, each 125g (4½oz)

200ml (7fl oz) olive oil, plus 3 tbsp

115g (4oz) caster sugar

2 tsp balsamic vinegar

salt and freshly ground black pepper

150g (5½oz) pea shoots

20g (¾oz) pine nuts, toasted, to serve

soda bread, to serve

Method

Method

1 Preheat the oven to 200°C (400°F/Gas 6).
Bring a saucepan of water to the boil, add
the large beetroots, reduce the heat, and simmer
for 30 minutes or until tender. Leave to cool,
then peel and dice.

2 Wrap the baby beets in a foil envelope with
the sprigs of thyme. Place in the oven and
bake for 15–20 minutes, or until they are tender.
Leave to cool, then peel the beets and cut them
into wedges.

3 Put the goat's cheeses in a bowl with half
the thyme leaves and pour over the olive oil.
Leave to marinate while you prepare the rest of
the ingredients.

4 Make a beetroot purée by melting the sugar
in a heavy pan on moderate heat. Then
cook for about 5 minutes until the sugar has
turned golden brown. Add the diced large
beetroot and cook for a further 3 minutes,
stirring until they are coated with the caramel.
Remove from the heat and add the balsamic
vinegar. Transfer to a food processor and
blend to a smooth consistency.

5 Pour the purée into a muslin-lined colander set over a bowl and allow the liquid to drain through. Season the liquid to taste and double the volume with olive oil to create a dressing. Also season the purée. Set them both aside.

6 About 10–15 minutes before serving, preheat the grill to high. Remove the cheeses from the marinade and blot off any excess oil with kitchen paper. Place under the hot grill and glaze the tops for 1–2 minutes, or until golden brown.

7 Place the pea shoots in a large bowl and toss with 4 tbsp of the beetroot dressing.

8 To assemble, spread a tablespoon of the beetroot purée on 4 plates. Add some dressed pea shoots and position a glazed cheese on top. Scatter over the remaining thyme leaves and drizzle around the remainder of the dressing. Add the baby beet wedges and sprinkle with the toasted pine nuts. Serve with soda bread.

Saffron-glazed scallops with apple and pistachio purée and pistachio oil

Dhruv Baker ⓜ champion

Preparation time 40 minutes   **Cooking time** 20 minutes   **Serves 4**

PREPARE AHEAD
Steps 1-3

Ingredients

For the purée

1 tbsp light olive oil

1 cinnamon stick

6 whole cloves

1 star anise

2 Braeburn apples, peeled, cored, and chopped

50g (1¾oz) unsalted pistachios, shelled

juice of 1 lemon

salt and freshly ground black pepper

For the oil

50g (1¾oz) unsalted pistachios, shelled

3 tbsp extra virgin olive oil

For the scallops

1 tbsp sherry or red wine vinegar

1 tbsp clear honey

small pinch of saffron strands

12 scallops, cleaned and corals removed

Method

Method

1 To make the purée, heat the olive oil in a pan with the cinnamon, cloves, and star anise, letting them fry gently for 2–3 minutes, or until they begin to release their aromas. Add the apples with 100ml (3½fl oz) of water and cook over a low heat for 5–10 minutes, or until very soft. Remove the spices and add the pistachios. Cook for about 5 minutes, then transfer to a hand-held blender or food processor, and purée. Pass through a sieve into a bowl, add a little lemon juice and season to taste with salt and pepper. Cover and set aside.

2 To make the pistachio oil, put the pistachios into a clean blender or a food processor, and add the extra virgin olive oil. Blitz in brief bursts, so the nuts are chopped, but do not form too smooth a purée, as you want some texture and bite. Spoon into a bowl, and also set aside.

3 For the scallops, heat the vinegar in a small saucepan until reduced to about 1 teaspoon. Stir in honey and saffron until well blended, and set aside.

4 About 10 minutes before serving, reheat the honey and saffron glaze over a low heat. Heat a large non-stick frying pan until searing hot. Season the scallops with salt and pepper and carefully place 6 of them around the edge of the pan, and cook for about 1 minute. Then turn over and cook for a further 1–2 minutes or until cooked through. Using tongs, dip each into the warm honey and saffron glaze on one side only and set aside to keep warm while cooking the remaining scallops in the same way.

5 Spoon 3 rounds of apple purée onto each serving plate and set a scallop on top, glazed side up. Spoon over a little pistachio oil, to serve.

Langoustines with green curry sauce and mango purée

PREPARE AHEAD
Steps 1-3

Cheryl Avery @ quarter-finalist

Preparation time 30 minutes   **Cooking time** 6–8 minutes   **Serves 4**

Ingredients

1 shallot, finely chopped

8 spring onions, cut in half

2 tbsp olive oil

16 raw langoustines, peeled

salt and freshly ground black pepper

1 small very ripe mango

4 tsp finely shredded basil leaves, to garnish

For the sauce

3 spring onions, chopped

1 fresh green chilli, deseeded and chopped

1 garlic clove, chopped

2 tsp finely chopped fresh root ginger

2 tsp coriander seeds, dry roasted and crushed

¼ tsp cracked black peppercorns

2 kaffir lime leaves, torn

1 stalk lemongrass, chopped

50g (1¾oz) basil, chopped

25g (scant 1oz) coriander with stalks, chopped

5 tsp olive oil

grated zest and juice of 2 limes

2 tbsp coconut milk

Method

1 First make the sauce. Purée all the ingredients except the coconut milk in a blender. Press the purée through a fine-mesh sieve into a small saucepan. Add the coconut milk and combine. Set aside.

2 Cook the shallot and onions in the oil over a medium heat for 2 minutes. Add langoustines, turn heat to high, and cook for 2–3 minutes on each side until just cooked through. Remove langoustines from the pan and season with salt and pepper.

3 Peel the mango and chop into small pieces. Place in the blender and purée until smooth.

4 To serve, warm sauce until just hot. Spoon some onto 4 serving plates. Arrange the langoustines and spring onions on top. Place some mango purée alongside Garnish with the shredded basil leaves.

Tian of crab with coriander-infused oil

Dean Edwards @ finalist

Preparation time 35 minutes   **Cooking time** 15 minutes   **Serves 4**

PREPARE AHEAD
Steps 1-3

Ingredients

200–225g (7–8oz) white crabmeat

2 tbsp crème fraîche

1 tbsp chopped coriander leaves

salt and freshly ground black pepper

1 large ripe avocado

juice of 1 small lime

For the coriander oil

¼ tsp turmeric

1 tsp coriander seeds

1 tsp ground cumin

1 tsp fennel seeds

1 tsp mustard seeds

1 stick cinnamon

4 cardamom pods

1 green chilli, deseeded

1 garlic clove, chopped

200ml (7fl oz) olive oil

35g (1¼oz) coriander leaves, plus extra to garnish

Method

1 To make the coriander oil, place a frying pan over medium heat and dry fry the spices for about 2 minutes. Add the chilli, garlic, and olive oil and allow to infuse on low heat for 30 minutes. Set aside.

2 Meanwhile, blanch and refresh the chopped coriander. Strain the oil and blitz with the coriander leaves in a food processor or blender. Pass through muslin and allow to cool. Place the oil in the refrigerator until ready to assemble the dish.

3 Mix the crabmeat with the crème fraîche and chopped coriander, and season to taste with salt and pepper. Mash the avocado and add lime juice, then season.

4 When ready to serve, place a 7cm (2¾in) ring mould on each of 4 serving plates. Spoon the mashed avocado and then the crabmeat mixture into each ring mould. Carefully lift off the moulds. Garnish with coriander leaves and then drizzle the coriander oil around the plates and serve.

How to prepare avocado

1 Hold the avocado firmly in one hand, then with a chef's knife, slice straight into the avocado, cutting all the way around the stone.

2 Once the avocado has been cut all the way around, gently twist the two halves in opposite directions and separate.

3 Strike the cutting edge of your knife into the stone and lift the knife (wiggling it if necessary) to remove the stone from the avocado.

4 To release the avocado stone from your knife, use a wooden spoon to carefully prise it away, then discard the stone.

5 Quarter the avocado and hold it very gently to avoid damaging the flesh, then use a paring knife to peel away and discard the skin.

6 To dice an avocado, cut it lengthways into neat slices, then repeat the cuts crossways to create the desired size of dice.

Sea trout with beetroot purée, mashed potato, and buttered kale

Alex Rushmer Ⓜ finalist

Preparation time 15 minutes   **Cooking time** 1 hour 20 minutes   **Serves 8**

| PREPARE AHEAD |
| Steps 1-5 |

Ingredients

2 tbsp olive oil

4 sea trout or salmon fillets, approx. 175g (6oz) each, pin-boned

knob of butter

juice of ½ lemon

sprigs of watercress, to garnish

For the purée

12 baby beetroots

small bunch of thyme sprigs

splash of olive oil

sea salt

splash of balsamic vinegar

For the mash

4 medium potatoes, chopped

100ml (3½fl oz) single cream

50g (1¾oz) butter

For the horseradish cream

1 banana shallot, finely diced

1 garlic clove, finely chopped

1 tbsp olive oil

250ml (8fl oz) fish stock

100ml (3½fl oz) single cream

1 tsp grated horseradish

For the kale

200g (7oz) kale

knob of butter, melted

Method

1 For the beetroot pureé, preheat the oven to 200°C (400°F/Gas 6). Put beetroot on a sheet of foil, add thyme and olive oil and season with sea salt. Scrunch up foil to seal, then bake for 45 mins–1 hour, or until very soft. Remove from oven, but keep oven on.

2 Leave beetroot to cool, then peel away and discard the skin. Put in a blender or food processor and whizz with a little vinegar to form a purée. Spoon into a sheet of muslin and squeeze out the juice into a bowl. Reserve the juice, put the purée into a clean pan, and set aside.

3 For the mash, cook the potatoes in boiling salted water for 15–20 minutes, until tender. Drain and press through a ricer. Heat the cream and butter and stir into the potatoes. Season well and set aside.

4 For the horseradish cream, cook the shallot and garlic in the oil for 5 minutes to soften. Add the stock, bring to the boil, and reduce by half. Stir in the reserved beetroot juice and reduce by half again. Strain into a pan and stir in the cream, horseradish, and seasoning to taste. Set aside.

5 Blanch the kale in boiling salted water for 6–8 minutes, then refresh under cold running water and pat dry. Set aside.

6 About 15 minutes before serving, put the 2 tbsp olive oil in a ovenproof pan to heat. Add fish fillets, skin-side down, and cook for 3 minutes. Flip over and add butter to the pan. Spoon over the buttery juices once melted, then put in the hot oven for 5 minutes to finish cooking. Squeeze over a little lemon juice.

7 To serve, reheat the kale, tossing it with the butter. Reheat the mash and divide between 4 plates and top with the kale, fish and warmed purée. Spoon warmed horseradish cream around the edge and garnish with watercress.

Lamb samosas

Daksha Mistry @ finalist

Preparation time 50 minutes   **Cooking time** 15 minutes   **Serves 4**

PREPARE AHEAD
Steps 1-4

Ingredients

250g (9oz) minced lamb

½ onion, finely chopped

1 garlic clove, finely chopped

½ tsp curry powder

¼ tsp chilli powder

½ tsp ground turmeric

¼ tsp ground roasted cumin seeds

½ chilli, finely chopped

1 tbsp chopped coriander

¼ tsp grated fresh root ginger

½ tsp salt

freshly ground black pepper

squeeze of lemon juice

1 litre (1¾ pints) sunflower oil, for deep frying

4 sprigs of coriander, to garnish

For the pastry

115g (4oz) plain flour

1 tsp salt

1 tbsp vegetable oil

about 3 tbsp warm water

Method

1 To make the pastry, mix the flour and salt in a bowl. Make a well in the centre and add the oil and enough water to make a firm dough. Knead dough on a floured surface until smooth. Roll into a ball, cover in cling film and set aside for 30 minutes.

2 For the filling, put all the ingredients except the oil and coriander sprigs into a bowl and mix thoroughly with your hands.

3 Divide the pastry into 6 equal pieces. Roll each piece into a ball and cover with cling film to stop them from drying out. Roll each ball of pastry into a 12cm (5in) circle and then divide into 2 equal semicircles with a knife.

4 Place a level tablespoon of the filling on one half of a pastry semicircle. Fold the other half over the filling to form a triangle. Dampen edges with water and gently seal them. Repeat for the other samosas. Set aside

5 About 15–20 minutes before serving, heat the oil in a deep pan. To test when the oil is hot enough, drop a small cube of bread into it. As soon as it sizzles, remove it and fry the samosas, 4 at a time, for about 5 minutes, turning occasionally, or until crisp and brown. Drain on kitchen paper, and serve 3 samosas per person while still warm, garnished with the coriander sprigs.

Pheasant saltimbocca with butternut squash and beetroot jus

Alex Rushmer @ finalist

Preparation time 25 minutes   **Cooking time** 1 hour 10 minutes   **Serves 4**

PREPARE AHEAD
Steps 1-5

Ingredients

1 large butternut squash, peeled, cored, and diced

3 tbsp olive oil

150–200ml (5–7fl oz) chicken stock

200ml (7fl oz) beetroot juice

2 sprigs of thyme

4 pheasant breasts, skin removed

salt and freshly ground black pepper

handful of fresh sage leaves

12 rashers streaky bacon

50g (1¾oz) butter, plus 15g (½oz) for the beetroot leaves

10 baby beetroot leaves, to garnish (optional)

Method

How to make chicken stock

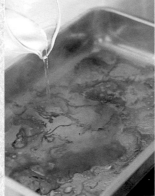

1 Roast chicken bones in the oven for 20 minutes at 200°C (400°F/Gas 6). This intensifies the flavour and colour of the stock.

2 Transfer the bones to a large saucepan. Pour 500ml (16fl oz) water onto the fat left in the roasting pan, and bring to the boil.

3 Pour the boiling liquid from the roasting pan over the bones in the pan, and add a further 2 litres (3½ pints) water.

4 Bring to the boil, skim off the foam with a ladle or slotted spoon. Add some carrots and onions, and simmer gently for 3 hours, uncovered.

5 Strain the contents of the pan into a bowl; you will find an extra ladleful of stock at the bottom of the pan. Discard the vegetables.

6 Leave the strained stock uncovered to cool, then use a ladle or spoon to skim off any fat that has settled on the surface.

Method

1 Preheat the oven to 200°C (400°F/Gas 6). Toss the butternut squash with 2 tbsp olive oil, place in a roasting tin, and cook in the oven for 25–30 minutes until softened. In a blender or food processor, blend the squash with enough chicken stock to give a smooth purée. Set aside.

2 Put the beetroot juice in a pan with the thyme, bring to the boil, and reduce to a glaze, which will take 5–10 minutes. Remove the thyme and set aside.

3 Season the pheasant breasts, place 4 sage leaves on one side of each breast, then wrap the breasts in the bacon. Wrap tightly in cling film to make a sausage shape and knot the ends. Poach in a large pan of gently simmering water for 10 minutes, then transfer to iced water.

4 About 20 minutes before serving, unwrap the pheasant breasts and fry in the remaining oil over high heat for 5–6 minutes, turning regularly until browned all over. Add butter to the pan halfway through the cooking time and baste the pheasant in the foaming butter. Remove from the pan, allow to rest, then slice. Wilt the baby beetroot leaves (if using) in a hot pan with the remaining butter.

5 To serve, place spoonfuls of warmed butternut squash purée and a scattering of wilted beetroot leaves on each of 4 plates, then position the pheasant slices, drizzle a line of warmed beetroot glaze down the centre, and finish with a scattering of the sage leaves.

Roast Moroccan lamb with couscous and harissa sauce

Helen Gilmour @ quarter-finalist

Preparation time 1 hour   **Cooking time** 30 minutes   **Serves 4**

PREPARE AHEAD
Steps 1-5

Ingredients

2 cannons of lamb, about 350g (12oz) each

For the marinade

200ml (7fl oz) olive oil

juice of ½ lemon

1 onion, finely chopped

3 tbsp chopped flat-leaf parsley

3 tbsp chopped mint

5 tbsp chopped coriander

1½ tsp ground cumin

1 tsp paprika

1 tsp sea salt and freshly ground black pepper

For the couscous

100g (3½oz) medium-grain couscous

6 dried apricots, chopped

50g (1¾oz) golden sultanas

25g (scant 1oz) salted butter

200ml (7fl oz) chicken stock

25g (scant 1oz) flaked almonds

20g (¾oz) mint, finely chopped

20g (¾oz) coriander, finely chopped

200g can chickpeas

25g (scant 1oz) nibbed pistachios

½ tsp ground cinnamon

3 tbsp olive oil (optional)

For the harissa sauce

3 tbsp rose harissa paste

2 tbsp plain yogurt

Method →

Method

1 Combine all the marinade ingredients, pour over the lamb, and set aside to marinate for a minimum of 2 hours, or overnight if you can.

2 Prepare the couscous. Place the couscous, apricots, and sultanas in a bowl. Add the butter and pour over the chicken stock, so there is just enough to cover the grains. Cover with cling film and set aside for 10 minutes to allow the stock to be absorbed.

3 Toast the almonds in a dry pan until golden and set aside in a bowl. Add the mint and coriander.

4 Fluff the couscous with a fork and add half the chickpeas and stir through. Add the almonds and herbs, and then the pistachios and

TECHNIQUE

How to prepare couscous

1 Place couscous in a bowl. Pour over about twice the volume of boiling water. Cover with cling film and leave for 5 minutes. Uncover, fluff up grains with a fork, then cover again for 5 minutes.

2 Now remove the cling film. Enrich the couscous by adding 1 tbsp of olive oil or a knob of butter, and season to taste. Fluff up grains again with a fork until they are light and separate. Serve.

mix thoroughly. Finally, add the cinnamon and season with salt and pepper, and add some olive oil, if required. Set aside.

5 For the harissa sauce, mix the harissa paste with the yogurt and warm it in a small saucepan over a low heat, but do not overheat as it may split. Set aside.

6 About 20 minutes before serving, heat a frying pan until hot. Remove lamb from the marinade, and cook in the frying pan for 8–10 minutes. Remove from the pan, cover with foil, and leave to rest for 5 minutes.

7 To assemble, divide warmed couscous between 4 plates. Slice the lamb, divide between the plates, and place a spoonful of warmed harissa sauce alongside. A spoonful of cacik (see below) is the perfect accompaniment.

Making cacik

Cacik is the Turkish version of the better-known Greek tzatziki. To make, peel and halve 1–2 small cucumbers, scrape out the seeds, finely slice the flesh into half moons, and put in a colander. Sprinkle with salt and leave for about 20 minutes for the juices to run out. Rinse, drain, and dry on kitchen paper. Mix 125g (4½oz) plain yogurt, a finely chopped garlic clove, and a small bunch of chopped mint leaves together with ½ tsp dried mint and some sea salt. Add the cucumber, stir together, and chill until ready to use.

Kyushu-style pork ramen with truffled lobster gyoza and aromatic oils

Tim Anderson @ champion

Preparation time 2 hours 30 minutes   **Cooking time** 10 hours   **Serves 4**

For the tonkotsu stock

1.5kg (3lb 3oz) pork thigh bones, broken

500g (1lb 2oz) pork spare ribs, broken

1 carrot

½ onion

1 leek

salt, to taste

PREPARE AHEAD
Steps 1-10

For the dashi

1 sheet konbu seaweed

2 litres (3½ pints) soft mineral water

80g (2¾oz) katsuobushi flakes

For the broth

200ml (7fl oz) dashi

400ml (14fl oz) prepared Tonkotsu stock

4 tsp soy sauce

4 tsp mirin

4 tsp sake

8 tsp water

2 tsp rice vinegar

20g (¾oz) dried porcini mushrooms

For the pork belly

rapeseed oil, for frying

250g (9oz) pork belly, rind removed

200ml (7fl oz) prepared dashi

200ml (7fl oz) prepared tonkotsu stock

200ml (7fl oz) dry sherry

200ml (7fl oz) root beer

100ml (3½fl oz) soy sauce

100ml (3½fl oz) maple syrup

For the noodles

8 tsp pilsner beer

4 tbsp rapeseed oil

2 eggs

1 egg yolk

150g (5½oz) "00" pasta flour

½ tsp salt

500ml (16fl oz) prepared dashi

Ingredients

For the gyoza wrappers

125g (4½oz) "00" pasta flour

1 tbsp rice flour

5 tbsp boiling water

For the gyoza filling

1 raw lobster tail, removed from the shell

10g (¼oz) fresh black truffle, shaved

1 tsp finely snipped chives

pinch of salt

pinch of white pepper

To assemble the gyoza

1 egg white

rapeseed oil, for frying

splash of sake

For the red aromatic oil

25g (scant 1oz) red miso

25g (scant 1oz) tomato purée

5 tsp rapeseed oil

2 tsp truffle oil

For the black aromatic oil

1 tsp rapeseed oil

4 garlic cloves, minced

1 tbsp Chinese black beans

2 tsp soy sauce

1 tsp black sesame seeds

5 tsp sesame oil

For the green aromatic oil

3 tbsp avocado oil

20 shiso leaves

2 spring onions, green parts

¼ tsp green yuzu-kosho paste

For the garnish

rapeseed oil, for deep-frying

reserved porcini mushrooms, well-drained and dried on kitchen paper

20cm (8in) rhubarb, cut into julienne strips 5cm (2in) long

4 spring onions, white parts only, cut into julienne strips 5cm (2in) long

16 enoki mushrooms, cut into julienne strips 5cm (2in) long

500ml (16fl oz) prepared dashi

Method

1 For the tonkotsu stock, place all the bones in a large stockpot and cover with water. Bring to the boil and cook for 10 minutes. Drain the bones and briefly rinse them. Return the bones to the pot and add the vegetables and about 4 litres (7 pints) of fresh water. Boil rapidly for 8 hours, frequently skimming the scum and replenishing the liquid with fresh water to keep it from over-reducing. Strain through a large sieve or colander lined with a muslin cloth. Season to taste with salt and set aside.

2 For the dashi, place the konbu seaweed and water in a large pan and leave to soak for 10 minutes. Bring to the boil, then reduce the heat and simmer for 10 minutes. Add the katsuobushi flakes and leave to infuse until all the flakes have sunk, then strain through a muslin cloth. There will be more dashi than you need for this recipe, but you can store the remainder in the fridge for several days or freeze it in convenient quantities for up to 6 months.

3 For the broth, combine all the ingredients in a pan and bring to the boil. When the porcini mushrooms have softened, remove them and set aside. Strain the broth through a sieve lined with muslin cloth. Set aside.

4 For the pork belly, heat the rapeseed oil in a casserole and sear the meat until golden all over. Add all the other ingredients and bring to the boil. Simmer for 2 hours, turning the pork occasionally, until the liquid has reduced to a sticky glaze. Leave the pork to cool in the pan, then cut into 3cm (1¼in) cubes. Set aside until ready to serve.

5 To make the noodles, beat the beer, 3 tbsp of the rapeseed oil, eggs, and egg yolk together in a jug. Combine them with the flour and salt in

a food processor and blitz until the mixture comes together to form a dough. Turn out onto a lightly floured surface and knead until smooth.

6 Using a pasta machine, roll the dough out into a very thin sheet and cut into fine noodles using the capellini attachment. Dust the noodles with plenty of flour to prevent them from sticking together.

7 Bring the prepared dashi to the boil in a large saucepan, add the freshly made noodles, and cook for 2–3 minutes. Drain, then rinse under cold water. Drain again, then transfer to a bowl and toss with the remaining 1 tbsp rapeseed oil. Set aside until needed.

8 To make the gyoza wrappers, mix all the ingredients together in a food processor and blitz until a rough dough is formed. Turn out onto a floured surface and knead until smooth. Roll out into a very thin sheet using a pasta machine and cut into twelve 8cm (3½in) circles with a pastry cutter. Dust each disc of dough with flour and cover with cling film to prevent from drying out.

9 For the gyoza filling, roughly mince the lobster meat and combine with the truffle and chives. Season with salt and white pepper.

10 To assemble the gyoza, add 1 tsp of filling to the centre of each wrapper, then brush around the outside edge with a little egg white. Fold wrapper over filling and seal the edges with a series of pleats. Repeat with the remaining wrappers and filling.

11 About 30 minutes before serving, heat a little rapeseed oil in a frying pan and fry the gyoza on one side for 2–3 minutes until golden

and crisp. Add a splash of sake to the pan and quickly cover with a lid. Remove the pan from the heat and leave to steam for 2–3 minutes, being careful not to shake the pan as this can damage the gyoza. (You may need to cook the gyoza in batches to prevent overcrowding the pan). Carefully remove the gyoza from the pan and set aside.

12 For the red aromatic oil, mix all the ingredients together into a thick, paint-like consistency. Set aside.

13 For the black aromatic oil, heat the rapeseed oil in a pan until smoking. Add the garlic and cook until charred, then add the black beans, soy sauce, and sesame seeds and cook until the liquid is mostly evaporated. Add the sesame oil and heat briefly. Transfer to a pestle and mortar and grind to a smooth oil. Transfer to 4 small dishes.

14 For the green aromatic oil, blend all the ingredients in a blender until very smooth. Transfer to 4 small dishes.

15 For the garnish, heat the rapeseed oil to 190°C (375°F) and deep fry the reserved porcini mushrooms until crisp. Drain on kitchen paper. Set aside.

To serve: Smear some red oil across the bottom of 4 deep ramen bowls. Arrange the pork cubes in a line bisecting the red oil. Pile the noodles in front of the pork belly cubes and set the gyoza on top of the pork. Arrange the garnish on top of the noodles. Transfer reheated broth to 4 small decorative teapots. Place one next to each bowl with a dish of black and a dish of green aromatic oil. Pour broth from the teapots into the bowls, then drizzle in the black and green oils.

Venison with red wine and blackberry sauce, and potato and celeriac mash

Polly Oxby @ contestant

Preparation time 15 minutes   **Cooking time** 40 minutes   **Serves 4**

Ingredients

For the sauce

400ml (14fl oz) beef stock

200ml (7fl oz) full-bodied red wine

1 shallot, very finely chopped

100g (3½oz) blackberries

2 tsp redcurrant jelly

For the potato and celeriac mash

1kg (2¼lb) Maris piper potatoes, peeled and quartered

300g (10oz) celeriac, cubed

100ml (3½fl oz) double cream

100g (3½oz) butter

For the venison

600g (1lb 5oz) cannon of venison

olive oil

salt and freshly ground black pepper

30g (1oz) unsalted butter

To serve

300g (10oz) purple sprouting broccoli

PREPARE AHEAD
Steps 1-2

Method

1 For the sauce, put the beef stock, red wine, shallot, and blackberries into a small pan, bring to the boil, then reduce the heat and simmer until reduced by two-thirds. Pass the mixture through a fine sieve into a clean pan and stir in the redcurrant jelly until dissolved. Simmer for a couple of minutes to reduce and make a lovely, glossy sauce. Set aside.

2 For the mash, boil the potatoes and celeriac in separate pans until tender, then drain. Mash the potatoes or pass through a ricer, add the cream and butter, and stir until smooth.

Place the celeriac in a food processor and blitz until it forms a purée. Combine with the mashed potato and season to taste. Set aside.

3 About 30–40 minutes before serving, preheat the oven to 180°C (350°F/Gas 4). Rub the meat with olive oil and season well on all sides. When oven is up to heat, place a frying pan over a medium-high heat and sear the venison until browned all over. Transfer to a roasting tin and smear with the butter. Roast for 8 minutes in the hot oven for medium rare. Remove from the oven and rest in a warm place before carving.

4 When almost ready to serve, steam the broccoli for 3–4 minutes until just tender. Slice the venison and serve with warmed mash, reheated sauce, and the broccoli.

TECHNIQUE

How to prepare celeriac

1 Holding the celeriac firmly on a board, then thickly peel the corm to remove all gnarled skin, using a sharp chef's knife.

2 Cut the peeled celeriac in slices, then grate or cut into chunks, dice, or julienne stripe as required for your recipe.

Mackerel on salt cod and butterbean salad with salsa verde

PREPARE AHEAD
Steps 1-3

Susie Carter @ quarter-finalist

Preparation time 25 minutes   **Cooking time** 5 minutes   **Serves 4**

Ingredients

8 mackerel fillets

olive oil, for frying

For the salad

200g (7oz) pre-soaked salt cod

3 tomatoes, deseeded and chopped

1 banana shallot, very thinly sliced

420g can butterbeans,

small bunch of flat-leaf parsley

1 tbsp capers

1 tbsp sherry vinegar

4 tbsp olive oil

For the salsa verde

1 large bunch of basil

1 large bunch of flat-leaf parsley

a few mint leaves

1 tbsp capers, drained and rinsed

6 anchovy fillets in oil

8 pitted green olives

1 large garlic clove, crushed

½ lemon, juiced

sea salt and freshly ground black pepper

olive oil

Method

1 For the salad. Drain cod and cut into thin slivers. Combine with the rest of the ingredients. Season to taste. Set aside.

2 For salsa verde, chop all the ingredients, except lemon juice, olive oil and seasoning, until finely minced and mixed.

3 Transfer to a bowl, then stir in half the lemon juice, a pinch of salt, pepper, and enough oil to give it a pesto-like consistency. Check the seasoning. If it is too sharp, add some more oil; if

there is not enough zing, add some more lemon or more salt.

4 About 10 minutes before serving, season mackerel. Fry, skin-side down, with a little olive oil over high heat for 2–3 minutes. Turn the fillets over and cook for a further 2 minutes.

5 Place a 7cm (2¾in) ring mould on 4 plates. Fill each mould with salad, then carefully remove the mould. Top each salad with 2 mackerel fillets and spoon a little salsa on the side.

Seashore and hedgerow

Tom Whitaker @ finalist

Preparation time 1 hour   **Cooking time** 40–45 minutes   **Serves 6**

PREPARE AHEAD
Steps 1-8

Ingredients

For the biscuit crumble

100g (3½oz) plain flour

1 tsp baking powder

pinch of salt

100g (3½oz) jumbo oat flakes

40g (1¼oz) ground almonds

40g (1¼oz) demerara sugar

75g (2¼oz) unsalted butter, softened

3 egg yolks

For the pudding

3 large gelatine leaves

25g (scant 1oz) dried carrageen moss, washed

250ml (8fl oz) double cream

1 vanilla pod, split open

6 egg yolks

100g (3½oz) caster sugar

100ml (3½fl oz) whole milk

3 tbsp agar-agar flakes

250ml (8fl oz) buttermilk

175ml (6fl oz) condensed milk

For the elderflower jelly

300ml (10fl oz) sparkling elderflower juice

100g (3½oz) elderflowers, washed

50g (1¾oz) caster sugar

4 tbsp agar-agar flakes

For the sauce

100g (3½oz) dried rosehips

100ml (3½fl oz) water

30g (1oz) caster sugar

3 tbsp quince jelly

To decorate

18 mint leaves

1 egg white, whisked

50g (1¾oz) caster sugar

2 tbsp pumpkin seeds

12 blackberries

Method

1 To make the crumble, preheat the oven to 180°C (350°F/Gas 4). Sift the flour, baking powder, and salt into a bowl and add the oat flakes. Mix the almonds and sugar together and add to the bowl. Rub the softened butter into the mixture, then add the egg yolks and mix until well combined. Line a baking tray with a silicone mat and sprinkle the mixture over. Bake for 15–20 minutes until crisp and golden, then set aside.

2 For the pudding, soak the gelatine leaves in cold water for 10 minutes. Place the carrageen moss in a pan with the cream and vanilla pod and simmer for 2–3 minutes.

3 Meanwhile, whisk the egg yolks and sugar together until smooth and creamy. Pour the infused cream through a sieve into the egg mixture and whisk to combine. Pour the mixture into a clean pan and heat very gently until thickened, being careful not to overheat the mixture. As soon as a the mixture forms a thick custard, remove the pan from the heat and immediately transfer the mixture to a jug or bowl.

4 Heat the milk in a small pan until simmering, then add the agar-agar. Simmer without stirring for 2 minutes, then whisk the mixture and simmer until smooth and the agar-agar has melted. Combine this mixture with the custard, then squeeze the excess water from the gelatine leaves and whisk into the mixture.

5 In a separate bowl, whisk together the buttermilk and condensed milk, then whisk into the custard mixture until smooth and fully combined. Divide the mixture between six 100ml (3½fl oz) dariole moulds and chill in the fridge until set.

6 Meanwhile, paint the mint leaves for decoration with egg white and then dust each side with caster sugar. Transfer to a baking tray lined with baking parchment and leave to dry in a warm place until crisp.

7 For the elderflower jelly, place the elderflower juice, elderflowers, and sugar in a heavy saucepan and simmer for 10 minutes until the sugar has completely dissolved. Strain the liquid into a clean pan and sprinkle the agar-agar over the surface. Simmer without stirring for 2 minutes then whisk and simmer for a further 2–3 minutes until the agar-agar has completely dissolved. Pour the mixture into a small plastic container to a depth of 1cm (½in) and transfer to the fridge for 30 minutes to set. Just before serving, turn the jelly out onto a clean chopping board and cut into 1cm (½in) cubes.

8 For the quince and rosehip sauce, bring the rosehips, water, sugar, and quince jelly to a simmer in a small pan and cook for 10 minutes. Remove from the heat and blitz in a food processor until smooth. Pass through a fine sieve and set aside. If the mixture is still a little grainy, add a dash of water and pass through a sieve for a second time.

To serve: Remove the puddings from the moulds and place at one side of each plate. Pour some of the sauce at an angle across the plate and scatter pieces of the crumble and the pumpkin seeds in and around it. Arrange cubes of jelly at the other side of the plate and top them and the pudding with the crystallized mint leaves. To finish, place 2 blackberries on each plate.

Chocolate cappuccino cups

Caroline Brewester @ finalist
Preparation time 20 minutes   **Serves 4**

> PREPARE AHEAD
> Steps 1-3

Ingredients

100g (3½oz) dark chocolate (70% cocoa), chopped into small pieces

300ml (10fl oz) double cream

2 tsp caster sugar

½tsp instant coffee powder

1 tsp icing sugar

2–3 drops vanilla extract

2 tsp cocoa powder, to decorate

4 crisp biscuits, such as cigarettes russes or langues de chat, to serve

Method

1 Put the chocolate pieces into a large heatproof jug or a bowl with a pouring lip.

2 Pour 200ml (7fl oz) of the cream into a small saucepan together with the caster sugar and coffee and bring it slowly to the boil, stirring occasionally. Then pour the boiling cream onto the chocolate and stir the mixture until the chocolate has melted.

3 Pour the cappuccino mixture into 4 small coffee cups or small ramekins and put in the fridge for 2 hours, or overnight, until it has set.

4 To serve, put the remaining cream in a bowl with the icing sugar and vanilla extract and whip to soft peaks. Spoon the cream onto the top of the cappuccino cups and dust with cocoa powder. Put the cups on saucers and serve with biscuits on the side.

Almond panna cotta with poached tamarillos and berries

Lisa Faulkner ⓜ Celebrity champion

Preparation time 30 minutes   **Cooking time** 40 minutes   **Serves 4**

PREPARE AHEAD
Steps 1-4

Ingredients

4 leaves of gelatine

250ml (8fl oz) whole milk

250ml (8fl oz) double cream

1 vanilla pod

50g (1¾oz) caster sugar

few drops of almond extract

For the tamarillos

100g (3½oz) caster sugar

1 vanilla pod

1 cinnamon stick

1 bay leaf

4 tamarillos, halved lengthways

For the berries

50g (1¾oz) caster sugar

60ml (2fl oz) cassis

50g (1¾oz) raspberries

50g (1¾oz) blueberries

Method →

Method

1 To make the panna cotta, first soak the gelatine leaves in cold water for 10 minutes to soften. Pour the milk and cream into a saucepan, split the vanilla pod and add to the pan. Bring to the boil, remove from the heat, and allow to infuse for few minutes. Shake off excess water from the gelatine and stir into the pan. Add the sugar, then continue to stir over low heat until completely melted. Take out the vanilla pod and stir in the almond extract.

2 Lightly oil 4 individual pudding basins that will hold 135ml (4½fl oz) of panna cotta then set them on a tray. Pour the mixture into each. Chill for at least 2 hours, or until completely set.

3 For the tamarillos, pour 200ml (7fl oz) water into a saucepan and add the sugar, vanilla pod, cinnamon stick, and bay leaf. Cook over low heat until the sugar has dissolved. Increase the heat and, when simmering, add the tamarillos and poach for about 5–10 minutes. Remove from the heat and leave to cool in the syrup.

4 For the berries, pour 100ml (3½fl oz) water into a saucepan, add the sugar and cassis and bring to the boil. Add the berries and cook slowly for about 30 minutes, stirring occasionally. The mixture should appear syrupy. Set aside.

5 To serve, dip the pudding basins in hot water for a couple of seconds then turn out a panna cotta onto the centre of each serving plate. Top with a berry and serve alongside 2 halves of a tamarillo and a spoonful of the poached berries.

Caribbean trifle glories

inspired by **Mark Todd** @ **finalist**

Preparation time 30 minutes   **Serves 4**

PREPARE AHEAD
Steps 1-5

Ingredients

15g (½oz) desiccated coconut

1 Jamaican ginger cake

½ small pineapple

4 tbsp dark rum

1 small, ripe mango

2 tbsp icing sugar

zest and juice of 1 lime

For the coconut ice cream

450ml (15fl oz) semi-skimmed milk

300ml (10fl oz) double cream

4 tbsp coconut cream powder

9 egg yolks

200g (7oz) caster sugar

Method

1 To make the coconut ice cream, put the milk and cream in a saucepan and bring to the boil. Add the coconut cream powder, stirring to dissolve. Remove from the heat and leave to cool slightly. Meanwhile, in a bowl, whisk together the egg yolks and sugar and pour the hot liquid over them. Return the mixture to the pan and allow to thicken slowly over a gentle heat, stirring frequently, until it coats the back of a spoon.

2 Allow to cool and, when cold, transfer to an ice-cream maker and freeze according to the manufacturer's instructions.

3 In a dry frying pan, toast the desiccated coconut until golden brown. Spread over a plate and leave to cool.

4 Cut the Jamaican ginger cake into 2.5cm (1in) slices and then into 2.5cm (1in) cubes. Cut the pineapple into 2.5cm (1in) cubes. Divide cake and pineapple between 4 sundae glasses and pour 1 tbsp rum into each. Leave to soak for at least 30 minutes, longer if possible.

5 In a food processor, blend together the flesh of the mango, the icing sugar, and the lime zest and juice. Spoon half of this coulis into the sundae glasses on top of the rum-soaked cake and pineapple.

6 To serve, divide scoops of ice cream between the 4 glasses, spooning the remaining coulis over the first 2 scoops and ending with ice cream. Sprinkle with the toasted coconut.

Dark chocolate mousse, green-tea financier, and milk ice cream

John Calton @ Professionals finalist

Preparation time 1 hour 30 minutes   **Cooking time** 1 hour 20 minutes
Serves 8

PREPARE AHEAD
Steps 1-10

Ingredients

For the ice cream

500ml (16fl oz) whole milk

500ml (16fl oz) ewe's or goat's milk

50g (1¾oz) caster sugar

100g (3½oz) condensed milk

1 tsp liquid glucose

1 leaf of gelatine

For the mousse

3 eggs and 3 egg yolks

300g (10oz) granulated sugar

3 leaves of gelatine

150ml (5fl oz) double cream

300g (10oz) dark chocolate buttons (60% cocoa solids)

3 tbsp vodka

600ml (1 pint) whipping cream

For the financier

125g (4½oz) egg whites

125g (4½oz) caster sugar

250g (9oz) butter

1 tsp matcha green tea powder

45g (1½oz) plain flour, sieved

45g (1⅓oz) ground almonds, sieved

1 tsp baking powder, sieved

For the chocolate leaves

400g (14oz) dark chocolate (70% cocoa solids)

For the coffee essence

300g (10oz) caster sugar

½ tsp liquid glucose

100g (3½oz) instant coffee granules

Method

Method

1 First make the ice cream. Heat the whole milk, ewe's or goat's milk, and caster sugar in a large, high-sided pan until the sugar has dissolved. Boil until reduced to 360ml (12fl oz).

2 Mix the consensed milk and glucose in a bowl, and pour over the sweetened hot milk. Mix well, then pass through a fine sieve. Leave to cool, then churn in an ice cream maker until set. Transfer ice cream to a freezerproof container and leave in the freezer until ready to serve.

3 To make the mousse, whisk the eggs and egg yolks in a bowl over a pan of hot water for 10-15 minutes, or until thickened and doubled in volume. Put 150g (5½oz) sugar in a pan. Heat slowly to melt, and then heat to 110°C (230°F), or "soft ball" stage on a sugar thermometer. Whisk into the thickened eggs and continue whisking until the mixture forms soft peaks.

4 Soak the gelatine in cold water. Put the cream in a pan and bring to the boil. Add the soaked gelatine and chocolate buttons. Stir until smooth, then add the vodka.

5 Whisk together the egg and chocolate mixtures. Leave to cool until about 20°C (68°F), then whip the cream and gently fold through until well incorporated. Leave to cool, then transfer the mousse mixture to a piping bag with a small nozzle. Set aside.

6 For the green tea financier, preheat the oven to 160°C (325°F/Gas 3) and grease a 23cm (9in) square baking tray. Put the egg whites and sugar in a bowl and lightly whisk to blend.

7 Melt the butter in a small pan, bring to the boil, and cook for a few minutes. Stir in the green tea powder, remove from the heat, and leave to infuse for 10 minutes.

8 Fold the flour, almonds, and baking powder through the egg white mixture , then add the butter and green mixture. Pour onto the prepared baking tray, and bake for 8–10 minutes, until just set and lightly golden on top. Leave to cool on a wire rack, then set aside.

9 To make the chocolate leaves, break the dark chocolate into and bowl, and heat over a pan of simmering water. When melted and smooth, pour onto a sheet of baking parchment on a baking sheet and leave to cool. Set aside.

10 To make the coffee essence. put caster sugar in a pan with the liquid glucose and 4 tbsp water. Heat slowly until the sugar completely dissolves, stirring occasionally and brushing the sides of the pan down with water if crystals form. Boil the syrup steadily until it begins to caramelize. Remove from the heat, and mix in the coffee granules. Cool, then pour into a squeezy bottle and set aside.

11 To assemble, cut the financier sponge into 8 equal-sized rectangles. Cut the chocolate into 16 rectangles, the same size as the sponge. Put 1 piece of sponge on each of 8 plates. Pipe 3 rows of the mousse onto each piece of sponge, and top with a rectangle of chocolate. Pipe on a further 3 rows of the mousse and top with a second chocolate rectangle. Place a scoop of milk ice cream alongside and spoon some of the coffee essence next to it.

Leave It Be

Slow-roasted duck with cabbage and gooseberry jam

Hardeep Singh Kohli @ Celebrity finalist

Preparation time 10 minutes   **Cooking time** 2 hours 5 minutes   **Serves 4**

| PREPARE AHEAD |
| Steps 1-2 |

Ingredients

4 duck legs

a few sprigs of rosemary

6 peppercorns

For the gooseberry jam

200g (7oz) gooseberries, topped and tailed

100g (3½oz) demerara sugar

To serve

1 Savoy cabbage, roughly chopped

knob of butter

freshly ground black pepper

Method

1 Preheat the oven to 200°C (400°F/Gas 6). Place the duck legs in a roasting tin and tuck in a few rosemary sprigs and peppercorns. Roast for 30 minutes, then cover with foil and turn the oven to 150°C (300°F/Gas 2). Cook the duck for another 1½ hours, basting from time to time. Leave to rest, saving the juices from the tin.

2 Meanwhile, place the gooseberries and demerara sugar in a saucepan with 2–3 tbsp water. Slowly bring to the boil, cover with a lid, and simmer for 20 minutes, stirring occasionally. Remove the lid for the last 10 minutes. The gooseberries will form a sticky, sweet jam.

3 About 10 minutes before serving, steam or cook the cabbage in boiling salted water for 4–5 minutes until tender. Drain and toss in butter and pepper.

4 Pile buttered cabbage on 4 serving plates, and put a warmed leg of slow-roasted duck on top, along with a spoonful of warmed rosemary-flavoured pan juices. Place a helping of the gooseberry jam on the side.

How to core and shred cabbage

Hold the head of the cabbage firmly on a cutting board and use a sharp knife to cut it in half, straight through the stalk end. Cut the halves again through the stalk lengthways, and slice out the core (which will be tough) from each quarter. Working with each quarter at a time, place the wedge cut-side down. Cut across the cabbage, creating broad or fine shreds.

Lamb stew with apple and sour plums

Mitra Abrahams @ semi-finalist

Preparation time 30 minutes   **Cooking time** 1 hour 45 minutes   **Serves 4**

PREPARE AHEAD
Steps 1-3

Ingredients

3 tbsp olive oil, plus an extra splash

2 large onions, sliced

800g (1¾lb) neck of lamb, cut into 2cm (¾in) slices

20 Iranian dried sour plums, soaked in hot water for 30 minutes

pinch of saffron

1 tbsp groundnut oil

2 apples, peeled, cored, and sliced into thin wedges

1 tsp ground cardamom

dash of rosewater

1 tbsp sugar

salt and freshly ground black pepper

200g (7oz) basmati rice

sprigs of chervil, to garnish

Method →

Method

1 Heat the oil in a large flameproof casserole dish over medium heat. Fry the onions until golden, then remove from the casserole and set aside. Fry the lamb in small batches until brown, adding more oil if necessary.

2 Stir in the onions and drained plums. Grind the saffron stems with a pestle and mortar, add to the casserole, and cover the contents with boiling water. Bring to the boil and simmer, covered, for 1½ hours.

3 When the lamb is ready, heat the groundnut oil in a frying pan, and sauté the apple wedges until lightly golden. Drain on kitchen paper. Add the apples, cardamom, rosewater, and sugar to the casserole of lamb. Season with salt and pepper and cook for a further 10 minutes. Set aside.

4 About 20 minutes before serving, put the rice in a pan and add 400ml (14fl oz) boiling water, a splash of olive oil, and some salt. Bring to the boil and simmer with the lid on for 15–20 minutes, or until cooked.

5 Shape the rice in a ramekin or cup and turn out a portion onto 4 serving plates. Arrange reheated lamb, fruit, and sauce next to the rice, garnish with some chervil, and serve.

Pheasant and parsnip fritters

PREPARE AHEAD
Steps 1-2

inspired by **Jamie Barnett** @ **Professionals quarter-finalist**

Preparation time 30 minutes   **Cooking time** 1 hour 30 minutes   **Serves 4**

Ingredients

15g (½oz) salted butter

1 tbsp olive oil

2 pheasants, ready to cook

1 onion, finely chopped

2 garlic cloves, sliced

4 rashers of smoked streaky bacon, chopped

2 dessert apples, peeled, cored, and sliced

1 bay leaf

1 tbsp sage leaves, chopped

200ml (7fl oz) beer

1 tsp light soft brown sugar

salt and freshly ground black pepper

100ml (3½fl oz) double cream

For the fritters

500g (1lb 2oz) parsnips, peeled and grated

1 egg, beaten

4 tbsp plain flour

½ tsp baking powder

15g (½oz) salted butter

1 tbsp olive oil

Method

1 Melt butter and oil in a large flameproof casserole. Add the pheasants and brown all over, then remove and set aside. Fry onion and garlic in the casserole until soft, then add bacon and brown slightly. Toss in apple and herbs, mix well, then stir in beer and sugar. Place the pheasants, breast-side down, back into the casserole. Season, bring to the boil and cover pan. Lower heat and cook for 1 hour, turning the pheasants over after 30 minutes.

2 For the fritters, mix the grated parsnips and egg in a bowl. Add flour and baking powder, season, and set aside.

3 About 30 minutes before serving, heat the butter and oil for the fritters in a frying pan and fry tablespoons of the parsnip mixture for 5 minutes before turning and cooking for 3 minutes on the other side, or until crisp and golden. Keep warm. Meanwhile, gently reheat the pheasants in the casserole.

4 Place pheasants on a warmed plate for carving. Stir cream into the sauce in the casserole. Simmer for 2 minutes. Slice pheasants and serve on a bed of the apple and bacon, with the fritters on the side and the beer sauce spooned over the top.

Rack of lamb with a cabbage parcel, shallot purée, and red wine jus

Simon Walker ⓜ Professionals quarter-finalist

Preparation time 55 minutes   **Cooking time** 1 hour 50 minutes   **Serves 4**

PREPARE AHEAD
Steps 1-3

Ingredients

2 racks of lamb (3 ribs each), trimmed of fat

1 tbsp vegetable oil

For the red wine jus

1.2 litres (2 pints) red wine

1.2 litres (2 pints) chicken stock

1 large bay leaf

few sprigs of thyme

For the shallot purée

150g (5½oz) salted butter

450g (1lb) banana shallots, chopped

300ml (10fl oz) chicken stock

150ml (5fl oz) double cream

sea salt, white pepper, and freshly ground black pepper

For the cabbage parcels

7 large leaves of Savoy cabbage, blanched

20g (¾oz) duck fat

100g (3½oz) pancetta, very finely diced

100g (3½oz) carrots, very finely diced

100g (3½oz) parsnips, very finely diced

50g (1¾oz) celery, very finely diced

50g (1¾oz) banana shallots, finely chopped

2 garlic cloves, finely chopped

few sprigs of thyme

Method →

Method

1 For the red wine jus, place a large pan on a high heat. Add red wine, stock, bay leaf, and thyme, bring to the boil, then reduce by three-quarters, which should take about 1 hour. Set aside.

2 For the shallot purée, heat a third of the butter in a pan, add shallots and sweat for 5 minutes. Add stock and reduce until all the liquid has evaporated. Finally, add cream and cook for 5 minutes. Place in a food processor and blend to a purée. Season with salt and white pepper, then strain and set aside.

3 To make the cabbage parcels, cut three of the cabbage leaves into julienne strips. Heat the duck fat in a large frying pan and add the pancetta. Cook for 5 minutes until crispy, then add the vegetables, garlic, and some thyme. Lightly cook and season, then empty into a dish and chill for

TECHNIQUE

How to French trim a rack of lamb

1 Remove blade bone by cutting under the skin along the edge of the cut. Slice horizontally from the skin, tight against the backbone, down to the ribs. Turn vertically and chop off the backbone.

2 Trim off elastin and any flank meat. To form the "rack", expose about 5cm (2in) of bone at the thin end of the ribs. Make a horizontal cut down to the ribs all the way across, and slice away meat above.

20 minutes. Place each remaining cabbage leaf onto a piece of cling film. Spoon a quarter of the vegetable and pancetta mixture onto each and wrap into a parcel with the cling film. Set aside.

4 About 45 minutes before serving, preheat the oven to 200°C (400°F/Gas 6). Season the lamb. Heat the vegetable oil in a non-stick frying pan, add the lamb and sear on all sides. Transfer to a roasting tin and roast in the oven for 15 minutes for a medium-pink finish. Leave to rest for 5 minutes.

5 Meanwhile cook cabbage parcels in a steamer for about 10 minutes.

6 To serve, arrange the shallot purée, cabbage parcels, red wine jus, and carved lamb cutlets on individual plates.

3 Remove the meat between the ribs by cutting down the length of the exposed portion of rib, getting the knife tight against the bone, then cut across and slice up along the edge of the next rib.

4 If serving two, a traditional method is to form a "guard of honour" by chopping the rack in two and intersecting the bones. For four, tie two racks of lamb together, skin-side in, to form a "crown".

Seafood tagine with flat bread

PREPARE AHEAD
Steps 1-5

Andy Oliver @ finalist

Preparation time 35 minutes   **Cooking time** 2 hours   **Serves 4**

Ingredients

2 black bream or 2 bream-sized red snappers, filleted with the skin left on and pin-boned, reserving the bones for stock

12 large raw king prawns (not tiger prawns), peeled, with heads and tails on

12 fresh clams

For the flat bread

250g (9oz) very strong plain or wholemeal flour, or a mix of both, plus extra for dusting

½tsp dried yeast

2 tbsp olive oil, plus extra for drizzling

sea salt

For the stock

fish bones

1 celery stick

small bunch of parsley stalks

1 slice fennel bulb

½ onion

2 bay leaves

6 fennel seeds

6 coriander seeds

6 peppercorns

2 slices lemon

2 star anise

For the paste

2 banana shallots, halved

2cm (¾in) piece fresh root ginger

2 garlic cloves

2 long mild red chillies, seeds removed

small bunch of fresh coriander, with stalks

½tsp ground coriander

½tsp ground cumin

For the tagine

2 bay leaves

1 cinnamon stick

2 tbsp olive oil

500g (1lb 2oz) waxy potatoes, preferably Cyprus, peeled and sliced

a pinch of saffron threads

100g (3½oz) medium purple pitted olives

2 large plum tomatoes, peeled and diced

4 small preserved lemons, cut into wedges, pips removed, reserving some for garnish

To serve

2 tbsp finely chopped mint

2 tbsp finely chopped flat-leaf parsley

2 fresh lemons, cut into wedges

a strong fruity extra virgin olive oil, for drizzling

1 First prepare the flat bread. Mix flour and yeast in a large mixing bowl. Gradually pour in the olive oil and 120ml (4 fl oz) water and stir slowly with one hand, bringing the flour into the middle until it all comes together to form a dough. Using the ball of your hand, knead until the dough is elastic and smooth. Alternatively, place all the ingredients in the bowl of a large electric mixer and knead using the dough hook until the dough is elastic and smooth. Shape into a ball, place in a bowl, cover with cling film and leave to rest for 1–2 hours in a warm, dry place.

2 To make the stock, place the fish bones, celery, parsley, fennel, onion, bay leaves, fennel seeds, coriander seeds, peppercorns, lemon, star anise, and salt in a large pan. Cover with 1 litre (1¾ pints) water; bring to the boil and leave to simmer gently for 30 minutes. Strain through a very fine sieve and taste. If it is too bland, return to the heat and reduce until it is more concentrated in flavour.

3 Make the paste by blending the shallots, ginger, garlic, chillies, fresh coriander, and ground coriander and cumin.

4 For the tagine, fry bay leaves and cinnamon in the olive oil in a large sauté pan or tagine

with a lid, add the paste and fry gently for 5 minutes. Add about half the fish stock, the potatoes and the saffron, and simmer for 20 minutes until the potatoes are nearly cooked. Set aside.

5 Meanwhile, to cook the flat bread, heat a griddle pan. Divide the dough into 4 equal pieces and roll each one out to about 5mm (¼in) thick. Rub the dough on each side with extra virgin olive oil and sprinkle with sea salt. Lay the pieces carefully on the hot griddle to grill for 3–4 minutes on each side until golden.

6 About 15 minutes before serving, add the olives, tomatoes, and preserved lemon wedges to the tagine. Add the remaining stock and season with salt. Lay the fish fillets, prawns, and clams on top. Bring to the boil, cover with a lid and gently simmer for 5 minutes, until the fish has turned opaque, the prawns are pink all over, and the clams have opened. Discard any clams that have not opened. Peel the skin off the fish.

7 Spoon the potatoes, seafood, and sauce onto plates, add the tomatoes and olives, garnish with herbs and preserved and fresh lemon wedges. Drizzle with extra virgin olive oil. Serve with the warmed flat bread.

Pears belle Hélène

Steven Wallis @ champion

Preparation time 20 minutes   **Cooking time** 20 minutes   **Serves 4**

PREPARE AHEAD
Steps 1-4

Ingredients

For the pears
1 tbsp caster sugar
4 bay leaves
3 cardamom pods
2 vanilla pods
2 Comice pears, with stalks

For the ice cream
300ml (10fl oz) double cream
200ml (7fl oz) whole milk
2 vanilla pods, slit, seeds scraped out but reserved
4 egg yolks
85–100g (3–4oz) caster sugar

For the chocolate sauce
1 tsp caster sugar
300ml (10fl oz) double cream
2 x 100g (3½oz) bars dark chocolate (70% cocoa)

Method

1 First make the ice cream. Pour the cream and milk into a saucepan. Add the vanilla pods and seeds to the pan and heat gently until steaming but not boiling. Leave to infuse for 5 minutes.

2 Whisk the egg yolks and sugar together until pale and foamy. Remove the vanilla pods and gradually whisk the warm cream into the egg yolk mixture. Return to the pan and cook, stirring, over low heat until a custard thick enough to coat the back of a wooden spoon forms. Transfer to an ice-cream maker and churn until set.

3 To cook the pears, pour 300ml (10fl oz) boiling water into a saucepan, add the sugar and stir to dissolve. Add the bay leaves and cardamom and vanilla pods. Heat gently to boiling point. Peel and core the pears, leaving the stalk intact. Add to the syrup, cover with a lid, and poach gently for 20 minutes, or until tender. Set aside

4 For the chocolate sauce, put the sugar in a pan with 1 tbsp boiling water and stir until the sugar is dissolved. Set aside. Warm cream in a heavy pan, add the chocolate piece by piece, and stir very briefly to melt. Remove from the heat and stir in the sugar syrup. Set aside.

5 To serve, slice the pears in half lengthways, then make vertical cuts about 5mm (¼in) apart. For each diner, scoop out a ball of ice cream the size of a small orange and place in a chilled deep dessert bowl. Carefully lift the pear on top and mould it around the ice cream. Set the bowl on a plate and serve warmed chocolate sauce on the side.

Chocolate and amaretto truffle mousse with a vanilla cream

Jaye Wakelin @ quarter-finalist

Preparation time 25 minutes   **Serves 4**

PREPARE AHEAD
Steps 1-4

Ingredients

2 tsp cocoa powder, for dusting

100g (3½oz) amaretti biscuits, crushed, plus extra to decorate

225g (8oz) dark chocolate (70% cocoa), broken into pieces

2½ tbsp liquid glucose

2½ tbsp amaretto

300ml (10fl oz) double cream

For the vanilla cream

150ml (5fl oz) double cream

½ tsp vanilla extract

Method

1 With a piece of kitchen paper wipe the base and insides of a 14cm (5½in) round, loose-bottomed cake tin with vegetable or groundnut oil. Tip in the cocoa powder and dust inside the tin. Tip out any excess.

2 Evenly sprinkle 75g (2½oz) of the crushed amaretti biscuits over the bottom of the cake tin and put to one side.

3 Place chocolate in a bowl over a pan of simmering water, making sure the bowl does not touch the water. Add the glucose and amaretto and leave to melt. Set aside.

4 In a separate bowl, beat the cream until thick. Fold in half the cooled chocolate, then fold in the rest. Mix until smooth and an even. Spoon into the prepared cake tin and tap tin to remove any air bubbles. Cover with cling film and chill for 2–3 hours, or overnight if possible.

5 To serve, whip the cream and vanilla extract together for the vanilla cream. Use 2 spoons to shape into quenelles. Remove mousse from the tin, cut into wedges and place one on each of 4 plates. Add a quenelle of cream and sprinkle over the remaining crushed amaretti.

Index

Acknowledgments

Shine TV and Endemol Shine Group would like to thank:

Frances Adams, David Ambler, Alice Bernardi, Martin Buckett, Claire Burton, Bev Comboy, Kerisa Edwards, Jessica Hannan, Ozen Kazim, Angela Loftus, Lou Plank, Lyndsey Posner, Franc Roddam, John Torode, and Gregg Wallace.

MasterChef alumni whose recipes and quotes are reproduced in this book:

Mitra Abrahams, Tim Anderson, Nihal Arthanayake, Cheryl Avery, Dhruv Baker, Jamie Barnett, Caroline Brewester, John Calton, Susie Carter, Sara Danesin Medio, Dean Edwards, Adam Fargin, Lisa Faulkner, Mat Follas, Chris Gates, Helen Gilmour, Lee Groves, Tim Kinnaird, Claire Lara, Linda Lusardi, Neil Mackenzie, Renaud Marin, Daksha Mistry, Andy Oliver, Polly Oxby, Wendi Peters, Alex Rushmer, Hardeep Singh Kohli, Dick Strawbridge, Mark Todd, Midge Ure, Phil Vickery MBE, Jaye Wakelin, Simon Walker, Steven Wallis, Kirsty Wark, Tom Whitaker, Cassandra Williams, and Gillian Wylie.

Dorling Kindersley would like to thank:

Libby Brown and Amy Slack for editorial assistance, Philippa Nash for design assistance, and Vanessa Bird for indexing.

Senior Editor Cécile Landau
Senior Art Editor Alison Shackleton
Managing Editor Stephanie Farrow
Managing Art Editor Christine Keilty
Jacket Designer Steven Marsden
Producer, Pre-Production Robert Dunn
Producer Stephanie McConnell
Special Sales Creative Project Manager
Alison Donovan
Art Director Maxine Pedliham
Publisher Mary-Clare Jerram

First published in Great Britain in 2018 by
Dorling Kindersley Limited, 80 Strand, London, WC2R 0RL
A Penguin Random House Company

Material previous published in:
The MasterChef Cookbook (2010), MasterChef At Home (2011),
MasterChef Kitchen Bible (2011),
and MasterChef Everyday (2012)

10 9 8 7 6 5 4 3 2 1
001—309619—Feb/2018

A CIP catalogue record for this book is available
from the British Library.
ISBN 978-0-2413-3336-5